Restitution in Criminal Justice

Restitution in Criminal Justice

A Critical Assessment of Sanctions

Edited by

Joe Hudson
Minnesota Department of Corrections

Burt Galaway
University of Minnesota

Lexington Books
D.C. Heath and Company
Lexington, Massachusetts
Toronto

Library of Congress Cataloging in Publication Data

International Symposium on Restitution, 1st, Minneapolis, 1975.
Restitution in criminal justice.

"Supported by the Law Enforcement Assistance Administration and the Minnesota Department of Corrections."
Bibliography: p.
1. Reparation—United States—Congresses. 2. Reparation—Congresses. I. Hudson, Joe. II. Galaway, Burt. III. Title.
KF1328.A7515 1975   344'.73'03288   76-43614
ISBN 0-669-00991-1

Copyright © 1977 by D.C. Heath and Company.

Published simultaneously in Canada.

Printed in the United States of America.

International Standard Book Number: 0-669-00991-1

Library of Congress Catalog Card Number: 76-43614

Contents

Acknowledgment

We are grateful to the contributors for providing a stimulating collection of papers; to Marlene Beckman, Law Enforcement Assistance Administration and Commissioner Kenneth F. Schoen, Minnesota Department of Corrections for their generous assistance; and to David Fogel for his early support and encouragement. This project was supported by grant number 76ED-99-0004, Law Enforcement Assistance Administration.

1

Introduction

Joe Hudson and *Burt Galaway*

The idea that persons who violate the law should be required to make redress to their victims has a long and interesting history. The concept is deceivingly simple to state, but it presents enormous difficulties for operationalizing in programmatic form. The terms *offender reparations* and *restitution*, as they are used throughout this volume, refer to a sanction imposed by officials of the criminal justice system that requires offenders to make redress in the form of monetary or service payments to either the direct victims of the crime or to substitute victims. In short, the concept of *restitution* implies the use of offender reparations as at least a part of the criminal sanction and involves some type of supervision of the repayment process by criminal justice officials. The papers in this volume trace the historical development of the concept, identify different cultural uses of restitution, and explore and assess some of the complex issues involved in operationalizing restitution programming at various levels of contemporary administration of criminal law.

The use of restitution within the administration of criminal law is neither new nor novel. Increasingly the concept is attracting renewed interest because of its potential utility at different levels in contemporary administration of criminal law. This book is one expression of that renewed interest. Later sections of this chapter will identify some recent legislative, policy, and program developments relevant to the idea of holding offenders accountable for making reparations to their victims.

First International Symposium on Restitution

The papers in this volume were first presented at the First International Symposium on Restitution held in Minneapolis, Minnesota, on November 10 and 11, 1975. The Law Enforcement Assistance Administration and the Minnesota Department of Corrections sponsored the Symposium as an expression of their continuing interest in the idea of offender restitution. The principle aim of the Symposium was to stimulate the conduct of more and improved research and program formulations. To a considerable extent, this has been an area in which individual scholars and practitioners have contributed as individuals, with little attempt to build on the work of each other. This volume aims at providing new

1

information and analyses to encourage the development of ideas and intellectual dialogues about program and policy issues and research needs and findings.

Current Restitution Programs

The paper by Bruce Jacob offers a historical overview of the role of restitution within the Anglo-Saxon legal system. The paper by Laura Nader and Elaine Combs-Schilling supplements the perspective provided by Jacob by presenting an anthropological analysis of the role of restitution within a variety of cultures. While these papers make clear that there are a considerable number of historical and cross-cultural precedents for the use of restitution, while its use has been suggested by a number of scholars,[1] and while the use of restitution was advocated at a series of international penal and penitentiary congresses during the latter part of the nineteenth century,[2] the use of restitution within the administration of criminal law has not received widespread acceptance or application. With the possible exception of its use as a condition of probation, it is only within the past few years that restitution programs have been developed at different levels within the criminal justice system. Furthermore, until very recently the use of restitution even as a probation condition received little attention or support from criminal justice practitioners. For example, the final report of the 1967 President's Commission on Law Enforcement and Administration of Justice makes no reference to restitution and only a single reference can be found in that Commission's *Task Force Report on Corrections*.[3] Even this reference is qualified with the caution that the practice of offender restitution may hamper the rehabilitation of offenders by infringing on their abilities to support themselves or their families.

Within the past few years a number of significant legislative, policy, and program developments that bear on the use of restitution have occurred. Iowa and Colorado, for example, have enacted legislation mandating the use of restitution. Iowa legislation enacted in 1974 requires that restitution be a condition of a disposition of either a deferred sentence or probation.[4] A restitution plan must be developed covering both the amount of restitution to be made and the payment schedule and then presented to the court for approval. The Iowa legislation requires restitution as a supplement to the probation or deferred sentence disposition and not as an alternative for offenders who otherwise would have been incarcerated; the disposition is made first and then the restitution plan is developed. An even more comprehensive piece of legislation was passed in 1976 by the Colorado legislature establishing the intent "that restitution be utilized wherever feasible to restore losses to the victims of crime and to aid the offender in reintegration as a productive member of society."[5] Under this legislation restitution may be ordered in conjunction with such sentences as incarceration in local jails, fines, probation, imprisonment, or parole.

In addition to legislative enactments, a number of national standard setting bodies have supported the use of restitution. The 1973 National Advisory Commission on Criminal Justice Standards and Goals identifies restitution as one of the factors warranting withholding a sentence of incarceration for nondangerous offenders and recommends that fines not be imposed when the fine would interfere with the offender's ability to make restitution.[6] The second revision of the Model Sentencing Act by the Council of Judges of the National Council of Crime and Delinquency explicitly recognizes restitution as a sanction to be used alone or in conjunction with other sanctions.[7] Restitution is also recognized in standards enunciated by the American Bar Association[8] and the American Law Institute.[9] Restitution is explicitly recommended as an alternative to prison by the 1972 Annual Chief Justice Earl Warren Conference on Advocacy in the United States.[10] The Law Reform Commission of Canada advocates the use of restitution and negotiated settlements as methods for diverting offenders from the criminal justice system.[11]

Restitution developments go beyond policy statements, however, and a variety of restitution programs have been implemented at a number of levels in the criminal justice system. In 1972 the Minnesota Department of Corrections established the Minnesota Restitution Center, a residential community corrections facility for adult male felony property offenders diverted to the Center after serving four months of a prison sentence.[12] At the Center residents are involved in completing restitution to the victims of their offenses. In addition, Georgia recently opened four restitution shelters.[13] These shelters are modeled partially after work-release shelters and receive probationers and parolees who live in the facility, work in the community, and make court-ordered restitution. Programs in other states and Canadian provinces are systematically making use of restitution in nonresidential settings, either as a condition of probation or as a formal part of a diversion program.

The editors of this volume were recently involved in an effort to identify and survey restitution programs within the United States and Canada.[14] Nineteen programs were identified in which restitution was a central program component. Staff of the 19 programs were surveyed to obtain information on program characteristics as well as the manner in which a number of operational issues related to the concept of restitution were being handled. The identified restitution programs were located in 13 states and 2 Canadian provinces: Six were under the administrative responsibility of departments of correction with an additional program administered by a state department of welfare having jurisdiction over juvenile corrections programs, 5 were administered by private agencies, 3 by courts or court services, 2 by the offices of city or county prosecutors, 1 by a sheriff's office, and 1 by another city agency. Of the programs, 12 were residential in nature with some of the residential programs also maintaining responsibility for clients after they had left the residential phase, and 7 were nonresidential in nature.

Of the programs, 13 served only adult offenders, 4 only juvenile offenders, and 2 served both adult and juvenile offenders. All programs serving juveniles were nonresidential in nature. The 19 restitution projects served clients at various stages in the criminal justice process. Five (3 adult, 2 juvenile) were primarily pretrial diversion programs; 4 served both pretrial diversion and probation clients (1 adult, 1 juvenile, 2 serving both adults and juveniles); 8 served primarily probationers (7 adult, 1 juvenile). A few of the programs for probationers also admitted parolees and 2 programs handling adult offenders served primarily parolees. No restitution program was being operated within the context of a prison, although a number of the adult residential facilities were work-release-type shelters, and some of the probation programs had contacts with offenders who had received sentences in local institutions as a supplementary sanction to the probation order. At the level of parole at least one of the programs made initial contacts with the offenders for the purpose of developing restitution plans while they were still imprisoned. The 19 operational restitution programs making up this survey population illustrate a diversity of administrative auspices and provide examples of both residential and nonresidential restitution programs operating at the pretrial, probation, and parole levels of the criminal justice system.

Further development of restitution programming for adults and juveniles has received impetus from recent federal initiatives. In 1976 the Law Enforcement Assistance Administration funded pilot restitution programs for adult offenders in seven states: California, Colorado, Oregon, Georgia, Maine, Massachusetts, and Connecticut. The Colorado and Maine programs are comprehensive and involve an effort to implement restitution programming at all phases in the criminal justice system. The program in Georgia will divert offenders from prison and probation to a program in which restitution is the sole sanction in the sense that the offender will be free of obligations to the criminal justice system when he or she has completed the restitution requirement. The programs in Oregon and Connecticut will implement restitution programming at the probation level for adult offenders. The California program will use restitution as a sanction for parole violators in lieu of their return to institutions. The Massachusetts parole board will introduce restitution programming into an adult correctional institution by integrating it with mutual-agreement programming and work release.

The Office of Juvenile Justice and Delinquency Prevention has just announced a plan to allocate $2,000,000 over two years to fund 8 to 10 restitution programs for juvenile offenders beginning in 1977. The juvenile restitution programs will be at the postadjudication level in order to test the application of restitution programming with more serious juvenile offenders. Both the adult and juvenile restitution projects are subject to a national evaluation; information developed from these projects will be useful in guiding decision making in future design and implementation of restitution programming.

The Growing Interest in Restitution

Given that interest in restitution programming is growing, what is contributing to this interest? One explanation can be found in two converging trends in American criminal justice, one of which is the rediscovery of the crime victim. The platitude that the victim is the forgotten party in the administration of criminal law is increasingly losing validity since there has been a recent flurry of activity centering on the crime victim. Manifestations of this trend include the emerging discipline of victimology, the adoption of public victim-compensation schemes in a variety of jurisdictions, and the increased funding for programs aimed at delivering nonfinancial, social, psychological, and advocacy services for crime victims. A commonly articulated purpose of restitution programs is to provide greater consideration to the crime victim within the justice system.

The second trend is the increasing dissatisfaction with current sentencing alternatives and contemporary correctional practices. The prison, once the shining hope of American criminal justice, is in disrepute and the bankruptcy of rehabilitation programs is being documented.[15] Consequently serious questions are being asked as to whether a thrust toward community corrections programming will provide either adequate public protection or fair treatment for the offender.[16] Restitution programming may appear particularly attractive in light of the growing dissatisfaction with currently available sanctions.

While restitution programming may be drawing its impetus from the rediscovery of the victim and the dissatisfaction with available sanctions, the implementation of restitution within the criminal justice system is a complex undertaking, and the idea should not be regarded as a panacea for resolving the many problems confronting the administration of criminal law. The papers in this volume address the complexities of restitution programming from a variety of perspectives, and, largely in common, they caution against faddish adoption of the concept.

Chapter-by-Chapter Overview

The papers in Chapters 2, 3, and 4 by John Stookey, Elaine Combs-Schilling and Laura Nader, and Bruce Jacob provide sociological, anthropological, and historical perspectives on the place of the victim and the role of restitution. Stookey's paper deals with the potential dangers inherent in the continuing neglect of the crime victim within the contemporary administration of justice. Restitution, as one way of addressing the needs of crime victims, is considered and largely found wanting because of the funneling effect in the criminal justice system—the volume of crimes committed as compared to crimes reported, as compared with criminal apprehensions, and as compared with convictions. To more effectively meet the needs of crime victims, Stookey proposes a combined restitution/compensation scheme. This proposal is similar to that made by Kathleen Smith in Chapter 9. In both proposals, a central compensation fund would be drawn on for crimes that failed to result in convictions, while convicted offenders would be required to make restitution to their victims.

In Chapter 3 Laura Nader and Elaine Combs-Schilling review alternative ways in which restitution sanctions have been applied in different cultural settings. The authors focus particularly on the implementation, functions, and purposes of this sanction as perceived by different cultural groups. Several points raised in this paper need to be carefully considered. What is the purpose of a system of restitution? Is it designed to benefit the victim, offender, legal system, or the larger community? Nader and Combs-Schilling note that in a number of cultural groups, restitution was used primarily for the benefit of the victim. They also note, however, that a number of additional purposes were commonly met: the prevention of further, more serious conflicts; the rehabilitation or social reintegration of the offender; the restatement of societal values; and the regulation or deterrence of potential offenders. A central question which then arises is the extent to which the potential purposes of a contemporary restitution program are compatible, conflicting, or operationally feasible.

Nader and Combs-Schilling also raise the important issue of the extent to which it is appropriate to have individual offenders make restitution to corporate victims when little practical consideration is paid to holding large corporations liable for the damages they do to individual citizens/victims. The authors forcefully argue for a broader view of what constitutes criminal behavior and the use of a restitution sanction for corporate offenders. They suggest that to fail to do otherwise is to continue administering justice from a model of "internal colonialism."

Another issue related to the question of the equal application of criminal sanctions concerns the extent to which restitution is ordered and used as an alternative to a more severe disposition such as imprisonment according to the socioeconomic status of the offender. Herbert Edelhertz in Chapter 5 notes in his paper that the less serious criminal offender is most commonly assigned the responsibility for completing restitution, primarily as a condition of probation. With the exception of some indirect and tentative data in Steven Chesney's work, we lack an answer to this question.[17] On the basis of structured interviews and review of court records, Chesney found that the most important factor in ordering restitution as a condition of probation was the offender's perceived ability to pay. Consequently, white, better-educated, working, and middle-class offenders were more frequently ordered to make restitution as a condition of probation as compared to members of minority groups with less education and from lower socioeconomic social strata.[18] The crucial question then becomes the relative extent to which offenders are given a disposition of incarceration as opposed to probation.

In Chapter 4 Bruce Jacob traces the historical development of offender reparations in Anglo-Saxon law and identifies some likely future directions for the contemporary system of criminal justice. Several major historical stages in the transformation of offender reparations are noted: private vengeance, collective vengeance and the blood feud, a system of composition or restitution, and the displacement of the system of offender restitution by the sovereign. In short, Jacob notes that the State assumed responsibility for and became the representative of the victim. The reason why restitution was displaced as a sanction in Anglo-Saxon law may not be attributed totally to the greed of the sovereign. The chapter by Jacob and the concluding chapter by Gilbert Geis make the point that the disappearance of the concept of restitution and the complete shift to the State's control over criminal law may have been a function of restitution causing some extreme hardships on offenders. In short, our ancestors' use of restitution may not have been as beneficent as some writers have suggested.

Chapter 5 by Herbert Edelhertz and Chapter 6 by Burt Galaway deal with issues relevant to the formal evaluation and assessment of restitution as well as the major legal and operational issues involved in the implementation of restitution within the criminal justice system. Edelhertz's and Galaway's papers complement each other in suggesting the need for careful research and empirical assessment before the idea of offender restitution goes the way of so many "innovative" ideas that have been implemented at different stages of the criminal justice system. All too often new practices have been tried briefly, oversold, and have taken on the character of fads prior to either being scrapped or institutionalized in a different, and usually corrupted, form. Then the next in a long line of fads takes its turn in the circular process of programming by fad. Both Galaway and Edelhertz caution against such an approach in the use of restitution and succinctly identify what is known, what knowledge is needed, and how to go about knowing it if responsibilities to the crime victims, offenders, and taxpayers are to be taken seriously.

Both Galaway and Edelhertz note that careful consideration must be given to the *purpose* behind a program of restitution. A common rationale often made by proponents of restitution programs is for the greater consideration of the crime victim; these authors note that such a rationale is, at best, problematic. In the survey the editors of this volume recently conducted of operational restitution programs, the project representatives were asked to specify the primary purpose of their program. Of the 19 respondents, 10 noted that the rehabilitation of the offender was the primary purpose, 4 indicated that providing reparations to crime victims was the primary purpose, 3 indicated that the primary purpose of the program was the increased efficiency and economy of dealing with victim-offender disputes, and 2 noted that the purpose was to change public attitudes and reconcile the victim and offender.[19] In short, existing restitution projects appear to hold a variety of different purposes; just over half the projects focused on the offender while approximately one fifth of the programs focused on the victim.

Program purpose will usually reflect the articulated goals or objectives of the program. Both Galaway and Edelhertz stress the need for conceptual clarity in the formulation of program goals and objectives. Galaway, for example, notes that carefully conducted evaluation research is directly contingent on the thoughtful formulation of program objectives and the careful specification and linkage of program components and activities with the articulated objectives. All too frequently program objectives or goals are stated in vague, global terms or, if articulated in operationally meaningful ways, are not relevant to the actual life of the program itself.

Chapters 7, 8, and 9 deal with alternative applications of restitution. In Chapter 7, Albert Eglash sketches out the idea of "creative restitution" as involving the requirement of some form of restitution by the offender to the victim which is effortful, constructive, relevant to the damages done, and leaves the situation better than prior to the criminal act. The close similarity of this type of restitution to the Alderian concept of "logical consequences"[20] is apparent from Eglash's paper and can also be seen as relevant to other approaches for dealing with people such as William Glasser's reality therapy[21] and the Skinnerians' emphasis on negative reinforcers.[22] Eglash particularly emphasizes the place of restitution in the form of service—either to the individual victim or the larger community. An example of the latter type of program is provided in Chapter 8 by John Harding. In this chapter Harding outlines and discusses the legal framework and organization of the British program of community services along with some of the major operational issues and likely future directions.

Several major issues run through all the chapters, one of which is the question of whether restitution should be made to the victim or to the larger community. Restitution to the larger community can be supported on the basis that crime is an offense against the State, and therefore the offender technically owes redress to the larger community. Simple justice for the direct victim of crime, however, would seem to demand that reparations be made to the party directly injured. Offender restitution to the community can be regarded as simply an extension of the original historical transformation of restitution paid to the victim into fines paid to the State. Harding's description of the British program of community service raises not only the issue of the recipient of restitution but also that of the form the restitution is to take. The British scheme clearly emphasizes offender service as opposed to monetary reimbursement. If restitution in the form of service is to be used, however, the question arises as to the recipient of service restitution. The direct victim could be designated to receive offender services, and this restitution may or may not be directly related to the criminal act—for example, repairing buildings damaged in the act of committing a burglary. Alternatively, as in the British scheme, substitute victims such as social welfare organizations could be designated to receive offender service restitution. From the survey the editors of this volume completed of operational restitution programs, service restitution appears to be a common form of restitution used on a frequent basis by 11 of the 19 restitution programs.[23] Clearly, however, the recipient of service restitution in these programs is almost always a substitute victim, usually some type of social welfare program or community-betterment group.

A related issue concerns the nature of the victim to whom restitution is to be made. The crime victim may be an insurance company or a large corporation rather than an individual citizen. What—if any—is the differential impact on the offender of making restitution to a large corporation as compared to an individual victim?

An additional issue raised in several of the papers is that of the direct involvement of the victim and offender in the development or ongoing completion of a restitution plan. Contrary views and practices appear in the literature and in operational restitution programs. A 1968 policy statement by the Canadian Corrections Association recommends that for adult offenders, an impersonal relationship between the State and the offender is preferable to direct victim-offender contact.[24] In contrast, Eglash's concept of creative restitution encourages the structured involvement of the two parties. Both the Minnesota Restitution Center[25] and the Iowa Restitution in Probation Experiment[26] encourage victims and offenders to participate directly in the formulation of a restitution plan. Such a practice does not, however, appear to be the typical one in existing restitution programs. A recently completed study dealing with the use of restitution as a probation condition in the state of Minnesota revealed that approximately 19 percent of the victims were unaware that restitution had been ordered. In short, nearly one fifth of the victims did not receive communication from officials in the criminal justice systems concerning the restitution order.[27] The recent survey conducted by the editors of this volume of operational restitution programs in the United States and Canada found that in only 5 programs was the victim usually involved with the offender in the development of a restitution agreement. Nine programs noted that such involvement only occasionally occurred, and 5 noted that it never occurred.[28] In addition, data from a study of Minnesota probation practices indicate that direct victim-offender contact is overwhelmingly discouraged by judges on the grounds that such a practice would be against the wishes of victims or might lead to further victimization.[29] Contrary evidence can be found to suggest that personal contact between victims and offenders may have the positive effect of minimizing the offender's use of rationalizations concerning the harm which has been perpetrated.[30] In short, while arguments can be made for or against victim involvement in a restitution program, little empirical support gained from operational restitution programs can be used to support either position.

The issue of victim responsibility also warrants consideration in a restitution program. Evidence is available to support the notion that some types of victimizations can most appropriately be viewed as involving the joint responsibility of both the victim and offender.[31] In some situations the victim may directly or indirectly precipitate the criminal incident. The issue becomes the extent to which victim precipitation should be considered in the assessment of damages and the ordering of reparations. The recent survey by the editors of this volume of operational restitution programs revealed that this issue was not considered by any program.[32]

The self-determinant sentence proposal made by Kathleen Smith in Chapter 9 is thoughtfully presented in relatively detailed form: Prisoners would be gainfully employed at a reasonable wage and expected to budget part of their income for restitution payments. Obviously, the major obstacle to such a program is the extremely low prisoner work-payment system operative in most—if not all—prisons. If one considers the fact that the vast majority of prison inmates committed for crimes against property have caused very small amounts of property loss or damage,[33] and if one further assumes that the federal minimum wage could be paid for inmate work, Smith's scheme would have the effect of drastically shortening prison sentences for property offenses. Clearly, until such time as prisons stop depriving inmates of the opportunity to work for reasonable pay, the use of restitution at this level of the criminal justice system will be an impossibility. Smith's proposal is clear in emphasizing that prison inmates would be afforded work and remuneration comparable to life in the free community. While she notes that vocational training programs, as well as educational and therapeutic activities, would be available to prison inmates on a voluntary basis during nonwork hours, progress in such programs would play no part in the releasing decision.

Smith's scheme for the self-determinant sentence should be viewed within the context of the current debate concerning the appropriate form and content of criminal sentencing and programming within correctional institutions.[34] While the specific purposes of criminal sentencing have commonly been stated in vague and contradictory form—to punish, to rehabilitate, to deter, to protect the community—recent writings tend to emphasize the punishment and deterrence functions as compared to prior emphases on rehabilitation. A relatively sharp break with the dominant paradigm of treatment and rehabilitation appears to be occurring within the contemporary administration of justice. More specifically, a movement back to many of the basic tenets of the classical and neoclassical schools of criminology is occurring along with a turning away from the central beliefs of the positive school. Within the classical tradition the emphases on people's rationality and ability to control behavior, the relative disregard of the question of causality, the stress on the deterrent value of punishment, and the essential freedom of people which is seen as in need of constant legal protection from the power of the State, are all becoming increasingly accepted. As compared to this emphasis, the positive tradition has stressed the role of causality and has sought explanations for criminal behavior in forces beyond the rational control of persons. The positivist regards criminal behavior as requiring treatment and rehabilitation rather than punishment and deterrence. Most commonly, such treatment and rehabilitative methods have been coercive, justified because of the social defense needs of society. Clearly, however, the assumption has been made that such coercive treatment is benevolent or nonpunitive in nature and consequently emphasis has not been placed on the role of procedural safeguards. On the basis of current writings and policy pronouncements, many central beliefs of the classical tradition are being increasingly accepted and displacing the emphasis on coercive treatment and rehabilitation. Smith's scheme for the self-determinant sentence appears to be quite compatible with the classical tradition inasmuch as it emphasizes the role of work, noncoercive-treatment services, and the protection of the due-process rights of offenders.

Writers from both the classical and positivist schools of criminology have advocated the use of restitution. For example, writing from a classical approach, Jeremy Bentham favored the use of a restitution sanction because of what he saw as its punitive aspects and what he regarded as potential deterrent effects that might result from its use.[35] A quite different perspective was provided by the positivist who regarded restitution as one of the three major components of their social defense proposals, along with the use of the indeterminant sentence and the classification of offenders.[36] Restitution was advocated by the positivists as one of the reasonable steps a society could take to defend itself from the effects of criminal behavior. Being heavy determinists, the positivists held that crime could not be prevented; however, they advocated restitution on the grounds that a society could reasonably require that, whenever possible, the offender compensate the victim for his losses.

Another issue relevant to restitution programming is whether restitution should be the sole penalty or used in conjunction with other sanctions. The papers by Nader and Combs-Schilling and Edelhertz address this issue from different perspectives. Nader and Combs-Schilling note that in a number of cultural groups, restitution was commonly used as a sole sanction. Edelhertz makes the point that in the context of the American legal system, the payment of restitution by the offender does not limit the right of the victim to pursue civil litigation and receive remedy as a result of such action.

There is another way to assess the issue of using restitution as the sole penalty or in conjunction with other penalties; should restitution be used in addition to such traditional sanctions as fines and imprisonment? Karl Menninger suggests that for at least certain types of property crimes restitution should be used as the sole penalty.[37] Quite a different point of view has been expressed by Stephen Schafer in his writings on the punitive use of restitution.[38] Schafer argues that the use of restitution as a sole sanction would have the potential effect of allowing serious offenders to purchase their freedom with a mild sanction relative to the criminal damages done.

Also relevant to this issue of using restitution as a sole sanction is the historical tendency in American criminal justice to supplement sanctions—usually with the rationale of providing coercive treatment or rehabilitation. Thus parole has been used to supplement imprisonment, probation to supplement a fine, incarceration in local institutions to supplement probation, with the potential effect of placing more people under greater degrees of social control for longer periods of time than would be the case in the absence of such rehabilitative programs. Paul Lerman's recent analysis of the California Treatment Project and Probation Subsidy programs incisively documents this point in relation to two of the more widely heralded community corrections efforts, and a sizeable literature on this issue is developing in relation to a variety of explicitly diversionary programs—from citation in lieu of arrest programs at the level of the police, pretrial diversion at the level of the prosecuting attorney, and judicial diversion to residential community corrections programs.[39] In each case, the crucial question is whether in the absence of the diversion program, the formally accused arrestee or convicted individual would have received the more serious sanction and, as a consequence, penetrated further into the criminal justice system. In restitution programming at the judiciary level explicitly aimed at diverting offenders from penal incarceration to a residential community corrections program, such a facility has an obligation to document that, in the absence of the program, offenders would have been incarcerated. Such documentation can best be provided through rigorous evaluation research efforts that rely on formally articulated program criteria to define the universe of eligible candidates. Even with such documentation, diversionary restitution programs are open to subversion that can result in expanding the degree of social control exercised by the State over the offender. The Minnesota Restitution Center's program, for example, was developed as an alternative to lengthy penal incarceration for adult offenders. Inmates were randomly selected from the state prison and released to the Center on parole status four months following admission. On completion of the agreed on restitution, staff initially anticipated parole discharge for program participants. However, because of the small amounts of damages done and the lengthy prison sentences received, the releasing authority was reluctant to discharge residents from parole once they had made full restitution. Consequently, Restitution Center residents were retained under parole supervision for periods in excess of the time it took to make restitution.[40] Comparing the total length of time under supervision (prison plus parole) for the two groups of experimentals and controls, the control group members were under formal supervision for a shorter length of time than their diverted counterparts who entered the Restitution Center. The parole board has apparently compensated for the brief period of time in prison for the experimentals by extending their time on parole. The net effect was that the diverted experimental group clients have been held under correctional supervision for longer periods of time than the nondiverted controls. The social control exercised by the State has been enhanced. The human and financial costs of such practices relative to the outcomes gained is questionable.

The Future of Restitution Studies

Given the recent popularity of the diversion concept and the growing interest in restitution, one would expect to find an increasing tendency to link the two concepts in operational programs. Whether, in fact, such programs actually act to reduce penetration into the criminal justice system is an open question. Such programs may be diversionary in little more than name only and actually perform as supplements to more traditional sanctions. This issue should continue to receive careful attention in both the theoretical literature and in the program arena. Perhaps the growing concern with the financial and human costs of coercive-treatment programs relative to the correctional gains that can be documented will result in an end of such practices. The issue is one of linking freedom to the offender's perceived gains received through appropriate participation in some form of therapy and is not one of whether or not to offer treatment services to offenders.

Another point that bears on the possible use of restitution as a supplement to criminal justice sanctions requires consideration. In restitution programs the restitution sanction can be displaced by other, more treatment-oriented activities such as various forms of individual or group counseling. The residential nature of many programs along with the nature of the clientele and staff feeds the tendency to mix program ingredients. By their very nature, the close supervisory and intimate nature of residential programs generate a concern with a host of personal, familial, and social problems held by clients in these facilities.[41] Being aware of such problems, the way is then left open for program staff to attempt to initiate ways to deal with such problems. The professional ideology of program staff can add further fuel to the intrusive character of residential corrections programs. Such staff have commonly been professionally socialized into an awareness and sensitivity to manifestations of intrapsychic and social dysfunctioning. In turn, corrections clientele can be perceived all too frequently as having an inordinate share of such problems. As a consequence, the restitution component of a residential program can quickly fade into insignificance in relation to the time, effort, and attention given to more explicitly therapeutic activities. The use of restitution in residential corrections programs may become little more than legitimation for coercively grubbing in the psyches of others. While not totally immune from such tendencies, using restitution within nonresidential contexts would seem to be less open to intrusion on the more personal aspects of offenders' lives.

The impact of the widespread use of restitution on various segments of the criminal justice system is a further issue for consideration. How will extensive use of restitution affect the phenomenon of plea bargaining? The possibility of restitution deterring prosecutors from dropping charges in a plea bargain because of potential adverse reactions from victims requires consideration. On the other hand, restitution may become a more central component of the plea-bargaining process as defense counsels encourage and support restitution in lieu of other potential penalties. In what ways will probation orders requiring restitution impact on the role and functions of the probation officer? Recent evidence from Minnesota indicates that while generally positive about the use of restitution as a probation condition, most probation officers were quite ambivalent about functioning in what they regarded as the role of a bill collector.[42] Increased use of restitution as a probation condition will likely result in changes in probation staff duties. More time may be required for communicating with victims, for arriving at a restitution plan, and for monitoring payments. In turn, this may result in decreased available time for more traditional probation practices, or, alternatively, perhaps the restitution and probation service functions can be integrated along lines suggested by Irving Cohen more than 30 years ago.[43] What are the implications for the criminal justice system of extensive victim involvement in restitution programming? Greater victim involvement may lead to increased overload on an already overtaxed system. At the same time greater victim involvement may generate increased public support for the criminal justice system or, alternatively, may lead to demands for reform in criminal law administration.

Notes

1. See, for example: Jeremy Bentham, *The Works of Jeremy Bentham, Now First Collected; Under the Superintendence of his Executor, John Browing* (Edinburgh: William Tait, 1838), Part 2, pp. 267-388; Herbert Spencer, *Essays: Scientific, Political and Speculative* (New York: D. Appleton and Company, 1892), Vol. 3, pp. 152-191; M. Raffaele Garofalo, *Criminology* (Boston: Little, Brown & Company, 1914); Enrico Ferri, *Criminal Sociology* (Boston: Little, Brown & Company, 1917); Giorgio del Vecchio, "The Problem of Penal Justice," *Revista Jurdica de la Universidad de Puerto Rico* 27 (1957-58), pp. 65-81.

2. Stephen Schafer, *The Victim and His Criminal* (New York: Random House, 1968).

3. U.S. President's Commission on Law Enforcement and the Administration of Justice, *Task Force Report: Corrections* (Washington, D.C.: U.S. Government Printing Office, 1967), p. 35.

4. Senate File 26, 65th General Assembly (1973), State of Iowa.

5. House Bill 1237, 50th General Assembly, Second Regular Session, State of Colorado.

6. United States National Advisory Commission on Criminal Justice Standards and Goals, *Corrections* (Washington, D.C.: U.S. Government Printing Office, 1973), p. 150.

7. National Council on Crime and Delinquency, Council of Judges, "Model Sentencing Act, Second Edition," *Crime and Delinquency* 18 (October 1972): 356-359.

8. American Bar Association, *Standards Relating to Sentencing Alterna-*

tives and Procedures (New York: Office of Criminal Justice Project, Institute of Judicial Administration, 1968), pp. 2.7(c)(iii); see also American Bar Association, *Standards Relating to Probation*, 1970, pp. 3.2(c) viii.

9. American Law Institute, "Article on Suspended Sentences, Probation and Parole," *Model Penal Code*, 1962, 301.1(2) (h).

10. Annual Chief Justice Earl Warren Conference on Advocacy in the United States, *A Program for Prison Reform* (Cambridge: Roscoe Pound-American Trial Lawyers Foundation, 1972), p. 11.

11. Law Reform Commission of Canada, *Working Paper No. 3: The Principles of Sentencing and Dispositions* (Ottawa: Information Canada, 1974), pp. 7-10; *Working Papers 5 and 6: Restitution and Compensation; Fines* (Ottawa: Information Canada, 1974), pp. 5-15.

12. Joe Hudson and Burt Galaway, "Undoing the Wrong," *Social Work* 19 (May 1974): 313-318; Robert M. Mowatt, "The Minnesota Restitution Center: Paying Off the Ripped Off," in *Restitution in Criminal Justice*, ed. Joe Hudson (St. Paul: Minnesota Department of Corrections, 1976), pp. 190-215.

13. Bill Read, "The Georgia Restitution Program" in *Restitution in Criminal Justice*, ed. Hudson, pp. 216-227.

14. Joe Hudson, Steven Chesney, and Burt Galaway, "Survey of Nineteen Operational Restitution Programs," unpublished, July, 1976.

15. Douglas Lipton, Robert Martinson, and Judith Wilks, *The Effectiveness of Correctional Treatment—A Survey of Treatment Evaluation Studies* (Springfield, Mass.: Praeger Publishers, 1975).

16. David F. Greenberg, "Problems in Community Corrections," *Issues in Criminology* 10 (Spring 1975): 1-33; Gilbert Geis, "A Halfway House is not a Home: Notes on the Failure of a Narcotic Rehabilitation Project," *Drug Forum* 4 (1974): 7-13; Paul Lerman, *Community Treatment and Social Control* (Chicago: University of Chicago Press, 1975).

17. Steven Chesney, "An Assessment of Restitution in the Minnesota Probation Services," in *Restitution in Criminal Justice*, ed. Hudson, pp. 146-186.

18. Ibid., pp. 167-168.

19. Hudson, Chesney, and Galaway, "Survey of Nineteen Operational Restitution Programs."

20. Rudolf Dreikurs and Loren Grey, *Logical Consequences: A New Approach to Discipline* (New York: Hawthorne, 1968).

21. William Glasser, *Reality Therapy* (New York: Harper & Row, 1965).

22. Cyril M. Franks, *Behavior Therapy: Appraisal and Status* (New York: McGraw-Hill, 1969).

23. Hudson, Chesney, and Galaway, "Survey of Nineteen Operational Restitution Programs."

24. Canadian Corrections Association, "Compensation to Victims of Crime and Restitution by Offenders," *Canadian Journal of Corrections* 10 (1968): 597.

25. Burt Galaway and Joe Hudson, "Issues in the Correctional Implementation of Restitution to Victims of Crime," in *Considering the Victim: Readings in Restitution and Victim Compensation*, eds. Joe Hudson and Burt Galaway (Springfield, Ill.: Thomas Press, 1975), pp. 353-355; Mowatt, "The Minnesota Restitution Center."

26. Bernard J. Vogelgesang, "The Iowa Restitution in Probation Experiment" in *Restitution in Criminal Justice*, ed. Hudson.

27. Chesney, "An Assessment of Restitution," p. 163.

28. Hudson, Chesney, and Galaway, "Survey of Nineteen Operational Restitution Programs."

29. Chesney, "An Assessment of Restitution," p. 160.

30. Ellen Berscheid and Elaine Walster, "When Does a Harm-Doer Compensate a Victim?" *Journal of Personality and Social Psychology* 6 (August 1967): 435-441; Ellen Berscheid, Elaine Walster, and A. Barclay, "The Effect of Time on the Tendency to Compensate a Victim," *Psychological Reports* 25 (October 1969): 431-436; J.L. Freedman, S.A. Wallington, and Evelyn Bless, "Compliance Without Pressure: The Effect of Guilt," *Journal of Personality and Social Psychology* 7 (October 1967): 117-124; J.M. Carlsmith and Alan Gross, "Some Effects of Guilt on Compliance," *Journal of Personality and Social Psychology* 11 (March 1969): 232-239; and Stewart Macaulay and Elaine Walster, "Legal Structures and Restoring Equity," *Journal of Social Issues* 27 (1971): 173-188.

31. Lynn A. Curtis, *Criminal Violence: National Patterns and Behavior*, (Lexington, Mass.: Lexington Books, 1974), pp. 81-100.

32. Hudson, Chesney, and Galaway, "Survey of Nineteen Operational Restitution Programs."

33. Galaway and Hudson, "Issues in the Correctional Implementation of Restitution"; see also United States Department of Justice, Federal Bureau of Investigation, *Crime in the United States*, 1974 (Washington, D.C.: U.S. Government Printing Office, 1975), pp. 26, 28, 31-34.

34. David Fogel, *We Are the Living Proof* (Cincinnati: W.H. Anderson, 1975); Norval Morris, *The Future of Imprisonment* (Chicago: University of Chicago Press, 1974); Ernst van den Haag, *Punishing Criminals* (New York: Basic Books, 1975); James Q. Wilson, *Thinking about Crime* (New York: Basic Books, 1975); Andrew von Hirsch, *Doing Justice* (New York: Hill and Wang, 1976).

35. Bentham, *The Works of Jeremy Bentham.*

36. Garofalo, *Criminology*; Ferri, *Criminal Sociology.*

37. Karl Menninger, *The Crime of Punishment* (New York: Viking Press, 1966), pp. 68, 190.

38. Stephen Schafer, *Compensation and Restitution to Victims of Crime* (Montclair: Patterson Smith, 1970), pp. 117-129; "The Proper Role of a Victim-Compensation System," *Crime and Delinquency* 21 (January 1975): 45-49.

39. Lerman, *Community Treatment and Social Control*; Robert D. Vinter, · George Downs, and John Hall, *Juvenile Corrections in the States: Residential Programs and Deinstitutionalization* (Ann Arbor: National Assessment of Juvenile Corrections, University of Michigan, 1975); Robert W. Balch, "Deferred Prosecution: The Juvenilization of the Criminal Justice System," *Federal Probation* (June 1974): 46-50; Joan Mullen, *The Dilemma of Diversion* (Washington, D.C.: U.S. Government Printing Office, 1975); Franklin E. Zimring, "Measuring the Impact of Pretrial Diversion From the Criminal Justice System," *University of Chicago Law Review* 41 (Winter 1974): 224-241.

40. Minnesota Department of Corrections, "Minnesota Restitution Center Preliminary Research Report, 1975," unpublished.

41. LaMar T. Empey and Maynard L. Erickson, *The Provo Experiment* (Lexington, Mass.: D.C. Heath, 1972), p. 91.

42. Chesney, "An Assessment of Restitution," pp. 161-163.

43. Irving E. Cohen, "The Integration of Restitution in the Probation Services," *Journal of Criminal Law, Criminology, and Police Science* 34 (1944): 315-321.

2

The Victim's Perspective on American Criminal Justice

John A. Stookey

It is almost a platitude to say that the victim is the neglected party within criminal justice administration. The major contention of this paper is that the very persistence of the American criminal justice system demands that it be more concerned with victims. We shall attempt to show theoretically the potential consequences for the criminal justice system of its continued failure to consider the plight of the victim; and we will argue that restitution in its present form is not a totally adequate solution.

Briefly, our argument is that being victimized will cause the victim to question seriously the legitimacy and usefulness of the criminal justice system. The rational behind this is that the individual will consider his/her victimization a consequence of the system's failure to serve its protection function. Therefore the unresponsive system is not worthy of support. We will further discuss the serious systemic consequences of such a feeling among a large victim population. Finally, we will argue that short of reducing the crime rate, which seems unlikely, the only way to regain the support of the victim population is for some means to be devised to make the victim "whole" again after victimization.

Most of the scholarly work dealing with the administration of criminal justice has centered on the plight of the offender. This is natural and appropriate inasmuch as it is the offender who may lose his freedom as a result of the criminal justice process. Concern for the offender is exemplified by the models of the criminal justice process that have been constructed, most of which follow the lines of the one developed by Abraham Blumberg, presented in Figure 2-1.

As can be seen from Figure 2-1, the offender is conceptualized as the hub of a wheel to whom all other agents and agencies in the system are related. Analysis of the other actors in the system usually takes the form of examining the way in which their behavior will affect the offender. For example, most literature about the prosecutor has dealt with the time constraints he faces and how these pressures affect the quality of justice received by the offender.[1] According to the literature, the prosecutor is pressed for time, and therefore the offender becomes the ultimate loser by being relegated to a mere number within an overcrowded bureaucracy. Similarly, study of the defense attorney has primarily discussed the job constraints of this position and how they affect the treatment of the offender. As with the prosecutor, the defense attorney is pictured as being motivated by organizational and time constraints. He must be concerned with

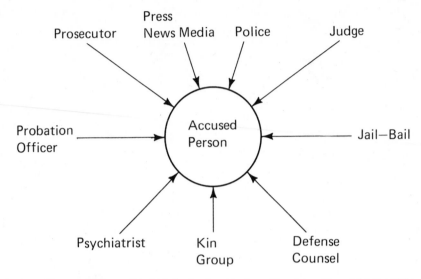

Source: Illus. p. 70 from *Criminal Justice* by Abraham Blumberg. Copyright © 1967 by Abraham S. Blumberg. Reprinted by permission of New Viewpoints division of Franklin Watts, Inc.

Figure 2-1. Model of the Criminal Justice System.

terminating as many cases as possible in the shortest period of time in order to ensure (1) an adequate income and (2) needed long-term goodwill with the prosecution staff.[2] In this instance, the offender is described as being betrayed and sold out not only the State, but also by the very person who is supposed to be his one and only protector; his attorney. Finally, research has revealed that even the arbitrator between the prosecution and the defense, the judge—the person who is to guarantee an impartial hearing—is motivated largely by organizational, rather than due-process, consideration.[3]

Clearly, the plight of the offender within the administration of criminal law has been studied from numerous perspectives. This is not to say that no further research is needed in this area. Manifestly, this is not the case if for no other reason than that almost all the work concerning the offender has been totally descriptive and devoid of theory. However, the near total devotion of criminal justice research to the offender has masked the fact that there is another consumer of the criminal justice system, the victim.

With the exception of some recent LEAA-funded projects and several sociological studies of the relationship between the victim and the offender,[4] within the criminal justice system the victim has been ignored. As a way of introducing a justification for consideration of the victim, we should ask why it has been only recently that this subject has ceased to be neglected. We believe that the reason can be found in the general growing concern for consumers which has resulted in a concomitant increase in concern for victims[a] as consumers of the criminal justice system.

However, while there has been growing concern for the victim, there have been no scholarly attempts to theoretically delineate the relationships between the victim and the other actors in the criminal justice system. We hope here to remedy this omission, for only if all the various relationships within the criminal justice system are elaborated can we fully understand the way in which the victim is treated in the postvictimization period.

Thus in Figure 2-2 we have borrowed the wheel analogy from Blumberg and applied it to the victim. Each spoke in the wheel indicates one of the actors or agencies a crime victim confronts as a result of victimization. In terms of the logical sequence of events, the first actor the victim comes into contact with is the criminal (A). After the perpetration of the crime, the next actor confronted by the victim is the police (B). After the police have concluded their investigation, the victim may then be linked to two other actors/agencies. The first is the court (C), where the victim may serve as a witness in his/her case or

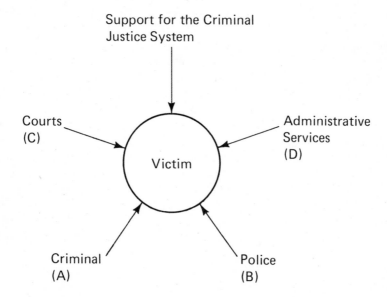

Figure 2-2. A Victim-oriented Model of the Criminal Justice System.

---

[a]Concern with the victim has been associated to a degree with the "Law-and-Order" movement. The argument has been that the system needs to care less about the offender and more about the victim. It seems clear that in many cases, this position was taken by politicians because they perceived it to be politically popular. Our concern with the victim is not motivated by such considerations but is given impetus by the desire to understand all actors in the criminal justice system.

attempt to use tort proceedings to gain payment from the criminal for damages and/or receive court-ordered restitution. Finally, victims may seek other methods of achieving services and/or reparations to compensate them for the effects of the crime to which they have been subjected. We have labeled this linkage "administrative services" (D). An example of this type of linkage is the existence in many states of compensation boards, which are administrative agencies that serve the function of allowing victims to petition for financial compensation for criminal loss. Additionally, there are various types of administrative aid given to victims in most states. For example, counseling for rape victims is a common administrative linkage between a victim and a governmental body.

As we have implied in relation to the wheel model of the offender's perspective, a mere descriptive analysis of the relationships between any consumer such as a victim of the criminal justice system and the components of that system does not tell us anything about the significance of those relationships. We suggest that the significance of the criminal justice system/victim linkages can be found in their impact on the victim's support of the criminal justice system. To explain this hypothesis, we need to borrow from general systems theory.[5] In systems terms, each of these linkages from the criminal justice actors/agencies to the victim can be considered a type of output from the criminal justice system that the victim consumes.

In its generic form, systems theory states in part that satisfaction with systems outputs will at least partially determine the degree of support for the system in question.[6] In the present case the output of the system is the nature of the postvictimization linkages between the criminal justice system and the victim. Support is conceptualized as the victim's support for the local criminal justice system. Thus if we can assume that victimization results in loss of support for the criminal justice system on the part of the victim, possibly the quality of the postvictimization linkages might be able to regain that lost increment of support. In other words, by making the victim partially or totally whole again, for example, by the police's recovering lost property or by the compensation board ordering victim payment, the criminal justice system may be able to regain the support it lost as a result of victimization. Thus on a theoretical level we suggest the significance of postvictimization linkages. That significance lies in the relationship between these linkages and support. However, the question remains as to why support is of concern. This requires the answer to two other questions: (1) Why is support of citizens *generally* important to the criminal justice system, and (2) Why is the support of victims *specifically* for the criminal justice system worthy of individual consideration.

Almost all studies of public support for judicial institutions have dealt with the Supreme Court.[7] However, we would argue that support for the local criminal justice system is of greater importance inasmuch as support for the Supreme Court would appear to have little meaning because there is usually no direct behavioral component to such support.[b] Conversely, there would seem to be some directly observable and important behavioral consequences that we might expect to vary with support for the criminal justice system. The local criminal justice system is to a large degree based on and perpetuated by lay citizen participation. Only with the help of witnesses, for example, can the courts and police (the primary components of the criminal justice system) effectively operate. Thus because we would expect that support would be related to the willingness to undertake this type of lay citizen behavioral participation, the concept of general support for the criminal justice system is significant.

In addition to the need for lay participation as a justification for studying support for the criminal justice system, it seems clear that in a democratic society support for a governmental institution is important as an indicator of the extent to which the system is meeting the needs of relevant populations. Support for the criminal justice system can be considered important because it is a monitor of the need to maintain the present system or reform it. This decision is fundamental to any democratic institution and therefore worthy of study.

As to the question of why support for the criminal justice system by victims is worthy of particular attention, the answer lies in the rapidly increasing crime rate. For example, a recent victimization study shows that about one out of every three households in urban areas has been victimized in the year prior to the survey. Clearly, it is not entirely the same group of people who are being victimized each year; thus we see that a majority of households in urban areas have been victimized in the last five years.[8] As the size of the victim population grows, its importance as a determiner of system persistence or reform becomes ever greater.

Given the importance of concern for the victim, the question then arises as to how well restitution meets this goal. As illustrated in Figure 2-3, restitution is not a very effective way of compensating the victim. Obviously, only a relatively small number of victims would be eligible to receive reparation under a restitution program. Therefore restitution in its present form is a very ineffective way of making the victim whole again or regaining victim support for the criminal justice system.

Given the failure of restitution schemes to meet the needs of the victims, we may ask about alternatives that might be more useful. The most mentioned and logical method is a State-sponsored compensation program that would not be tied to the apprehension of the offender or the offender's ability to pay. This type of program would clearly best meet the needs of the victim. It may be

---

[b]This is not to say that support for the Supreme Court has no behavioral component. Expressions of public opinion are often made as a result of its decreasing support for the system. For example, it seems clear that public opinion against the economic conservation decisions of the 1936-37 Court led in part to the "switch in time that saved nine." Our contention here is merely that in *most* cases there is not a behavioral component to support for the Supreme Court.

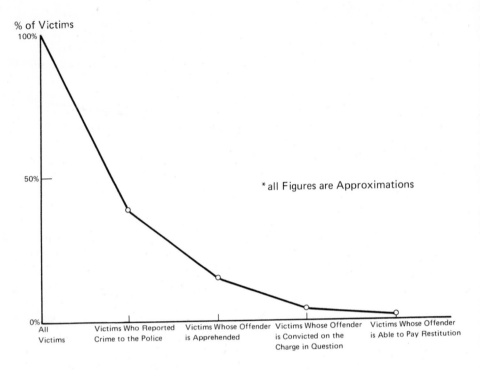

% of Victims

Figure 2-3. Funneling Effects of Criminal Justice Process.

asked, however, what effect this type of program would have on the rehabilitative functions of restitution. While a strict compensation program would eliminate the participation of the offender, a hybrid somewhere between the pure models of compensation and restitution could be developed. If the offender were caught and could afford to pay, a restitution program would be used. In other circumstances the State compensation program would be used.

A compensation program would allow for the immediate payment of the victim in all cases. As soon as a victimization has been determined, the compensation board could pay the victim. If the offender were caught and were able to pay, then the offender could be ordered to pay restitution to the compensation board as some offenders are now ordered to pay restitution to insurance companies. In this way the rehabilitative goals of restitution could be maintained along with the goal of compensating the victim.

In conclusion, we would argue that increased concern for the victim is a necessity if the present criminal justice system is to persist. Additionally, it seems clear that restitution in its present form does not meet this need. Therefore we urge that alternative means be developed and tested that would allow for both rehabilitation of the offender and compensation for the victim.

Notes

1. For example, see A. Alschuler, "The Prosecutor's Role in Plea Bargaining," *University of Chicago Law Review* 36 (1968): 50; George Cole, "Decision to Prosecute," *Law and Society Review* 4 (1970): 331.

2. Abraham S. Blumberg, "The Practice of Law as a Confidence Game: Organizational Cooptation of a Profession," *Law and Society Review* 1 (1967): 15; A. Battle, "In Search of the Adversary System—The Cooperative Practices of Private Defense Attorneys," *Texas Law Review* 50 (1971): 60.

3. George Cole, *Politics and the Administration of Justice* (Beverly Hills, Calif.: Sage Publications, 1973), p. 195; Abraham Blumberg, *Criminal Justice* (Chicago: Quadrangle, 1970), pp. 117-142.

4. For example, see United States Department of Justice, Law Enforcement Assistance Administration, *Criminal Victimization Surveys in the Nation's Five Largest Cities* (Washington, D.C.: U.S. Government Printing Office, 1974); United States President's Commission on Law Enforcement and Administration of Justice, *Task Force Report: Crime and It's Impact—An Assessment* (Washington, D.C.: U.S. Government Printing Office, 1967); Marvin E. Wolfgang, "Victim-Precipitated Criminal Homicide," *Journal of Criminal Law, Criminology and Police Science* 48 (1975): 1; Michael Fooner, "Victim Induced Criminality," *Science* (1966): 1080.

5. For a general discussion of the systems model, see David Easton, *A Systems Analysis of Political Life* (New York: Wiley, 1965).

6. David Easton, *A Framework for Political Analysis* (Englewood Cliffs, N.J.: Prentice-Hall, 1965) p. 124.

7. For an example of studies of support for the Supreme Court, see Walter Murphy and Joseph Tanenhaus, "Public Opinion and the U.S. Supreme Court," in *Frontiers of Judicial Research* Joseph Tanenhaus and Joel Grossman eds. (New York: Wiley, 1968), p. 273.

8. *Criminal Justice Digest* 3 (August 1975): 9.

3 Restitution in Cross-cultural Perspective

Laura Nader and
Elaine Combs-Schilling

This paper will illustrate how the restitution process works in certain non-Western societies, to what aims and purposes it works, and in what variations it may appear. In the discussion at the end of this paper, we will deal with the question of whether such information is of any practical use to those interested in expanding the use of restitution as a sanctioning mechanism in modern Western socity. It is expected that a knowledge of *process* and of the various types of restitution schemes in other societies will alert us to the importance of a contextual or ethnographic perspective whereby we see restitution programs in a wider scope than that of merely an additional program for managing lower-income criminals.

We should like to stress that we believe the historical perspective is important, if well constructed, to understand how, why, and where restitution has changed over time. In addition, we would like to caution the reader that many of the references people make to restitution in past or contemporary primitive or preliterate societies are just plain wrong or full of misconceptions. As we shall illustrate, it is important to realize these errors in part because "other societies" are often used as justification for what we do or as illustration that something is "natural" since it appears to be universal. For example, although it is widely held to be true, it is unlikely that the "eye-for-an-eye" theory ever really held for preliterate people. It is not retaliation but rather a desire to replace the loss with damages that characterizes preliterates. And still today it is restitution, not social retaliation or retribution, that is widespread.

A few more words about the literature in anthropology may help those who wish to go beyond this paper. Materials on compensation or restitution are scattered in anthropological monographs. There is often no reference to the subject matter in the indexes. The topic is usually discussed in conjunction with sanctions used in law, supernatural systems, or in other social-control processes. Restitution is also discussed in reference to kinship or political systems that may influence whether they are disbursed by the offending party or by the State. Materials are often found embedded in case materials.

Terms are important to agree on. We warn the reader of anthropological materials that terms such as *restitution, compensation,* and *damages* may be used interchangeably. In this paper we will respect the usage presently accepted in America, whereby compensation refers to monies or services paid by the *State* to the victim or, we might add, by the offender to the State. Restitution refers to monies or services paid by the *offender* to the victim, whether directly to the victim or through intermediaries such as insurance companies. The term *symbolic restitution* is confusing, and we suggest it be dropped; restitution or compensation can be made in money or in service terms (see Figure 3-1).

It is important to explore the non-Western literature for living laboratory examples of how restitution works *in situ*. In this paper we will discuss examples as ideal types. The components of the restitution process we emphasize are the following: (1) the dominant liability pattern, i.e., collective or individual; (2) the nature of the crimes or acts for which restitution was applicable; (3) the critical determinants of the type and amount of restitution—whether in kind (e.g., a life for a life) or equivalence (a wife for a life); (4) the process by which a given restitution is agreed on; who pays, to whom it is paid, and who shares in the process; and (5) the functions of the restitution process.

Restitution in Societies with Collective Liability

Let us begin with a brief descriptive sketch of the system of reparation as found among the Berber tribes of the Middle Atlas Mountains of Morocco. This system of restitution is illustrative of that in societies where liability is predominantly collective. These tribes were most recently studied by Ernest Gellner. His findings are published in the book *Saints of the Atlas* (1969). The case of murder will serve as illustration, as the process of arriving at a settlement to a murder case is representative of the process used, in varying degrees, in other serious cases of rule breaking.

The Process

If a murder were committed, it might immediately be followed by retaliation, but this reaction was typically avoided, especially by those in frequent social contact, as its destructive aspects (i.e., the feud) were often perceived by all parties concerned as mutually destructive. Traditionally, murder was followed by the flight of the murderer and ten agnates. "This flight would aim at safety

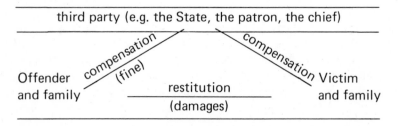

Figure 3-1.

by distance, or by flight to the tribes' traditional enemies, or to the sanctuary of the saints."[1] The flight to the sanctuary of the saints was particularly advantageous, as the saints' household was considered a sacred place where no blood could be shed without the offender incurring the severest of earthly and supernatural sanctions. Refuge in the saints' household was also advantageous from the standpoint that it was the saints who began negotiation proceedings, and it was on their sacred property that negotiations were carried out. The saints in the Berber tribes were and are believed to be descendents of the Prophet and endowed by Allah with supernatural powers. One of the most important functions of saintly shrines was to provide sanctuary that worked in two ways for dispute settlement: (1) They were secure places where rival tribes or groups in conflict could meet to negotiate in safety, and (2) the lodges were safe places for murderers and their kin during the period before blood-money had been agreed to and accepted.[2]

After an initial "cooling-off" period, negotiations would be opened through the saints. After some days the group of the murdered person would allow the family of the killer, though not the killer, to return home. Next came the prolonged period of negotiations with the saint serving as mediator between the group of the victim and the group of the offender.

If the murderer admitted guilt, then the question of the amount of compensation due the victim's group could immediately be considered. If not, there was a complex procedure of collective oath taking at the saints' shrine that would be used to determine guilt. Once the question of guilt was determined, negotiations would center on the amount of reparation to be paid to the victim's family. The status of the victim as well as the type of crime committed were the most important variables in determining the appropriate sum.

Finally, the victim's family and the offender's family would agree on the amount of compensation. Peace would be restored when the amount of compensation was paid. Usually the murderer was also exiled, a condition that the group whose member had been killed might later reverse. The rule governing the payment and distribution of blood-money was that the culprit pays one half, and the rest of his close agnates pay the remaining half, while the sons (or if no sons, the brothers) of the murdered person receive one half, and his close agnates, the other half.[3]

If in the negotiation process, no amount of compensation were agreed on, the family of the victim had the alternative of resorting to the feud to sanction the offender and his family. However, this alternative was seldom resorted to, as its consequences tended to be mutually destructive for all parties concerned. (As Gellner states, the direct resort to violence was feasible only for larger and more distant groups.[4]) The threat of the feud, in and of itself, served as one of the most powerful sanctions for bringing about compromise, for inducing the parties to settle on a mutually acceptable amount of reparation. Evans-Pritchard, in his study of the Nuer draws this same conclusion.[5] Colson, in her extensive review of the literature on the feud, notes the pervasiveness of the threat of the feud serving as a powerful force for compromise and peaceful settlement among disputing parties in traditional societies.[6]

The Components

In this section we will briefly look at the main components of the restitution process among the tribes of the Middle Atlas, noting some of the variation in procedure that exists in other traditional societies. No attempt is made to be comprehensive; rather we have chosen societies that highlight the most important variables in the restitution process. Those readers familiar with the anthropological literature will have already noted that the settlement process described above is similar to that described by Evans-Pritchard in his classic study of the *Nuer*, a segmentary tribal group in the Sudan.[7] Among the Nuer, the leopard-skin chief occupied a structural position much like that of the saint of the Middle Atlas. He too was a sacred figure, endowed with supernatural powers. It was to him that rule breakers, especially murderers, fled to find sanctuary.

The main components of both of the preceding restitution systems follow.

1. *The Committing of the rule-breaking act.*

2. *A "cooling-off" period with some mechanism for the culprit's refuge while the case was being evaluated.* As noted among the Middle Atlas tribes and among the Nuer, the culprit, with close kinsmen, fled to the households of the sacred leaders (the saints or the leopard-skin chiefs) where they were provided with sanctuary. Among tribes lacking sacred leaders who provided sanctuary, other mechanisms existed to provide for the safety of the culprit during the cooling-off period. The culprit and his close kinsmen might flee the area entirely, or, as among the Tong of Zambia, there might be an initial period of severance of all social relations between the family of the victim and the family of the offender.[8] Members of the two groups would scrupulously avoid one another until negotiations for settlement of the dispute began, an effective way of avoiding immediate resort to retaliatory violence.

3. *A period of negotiation between the two parties of the dispute to arrive at some mutually acceptable compensation.* The *period of negotiation* between the victim's and the offender's groups (often kin-based groups) can be conducted either (1) by specialized mediating personnel or (2) by the concerned parties themselves. As noted, the Nuer and the Middle Atlas tribes have permanent specialized mediating personnel while the Ifugao have a "go-between" selected for each separate conflict by the two parties themselves.[9] Among the Yurok of California[10] and among the Tonga of Zambia,[11] negotiations are carried out by members of the disputing parties themselves. It is those people who have cross-cutting ties with both groups who typically begin the negotiations. This is illustrated by the case of the Tonga cited above.[12] As we noted initially, all social relations between the offending and the offended parties would be severed. This situation proved most difficult for those with close ties to both groups, e.g., a woman who was member of the culprit's clan but the wife of a

man in the victim's clan. Because clan membership was the determining criteria of ultimate allegiance in this society, the woman was forced to sever her social relations with her husband and his kinsmen. Needless to say, she was anxious to get the dispute settled so that she could resume normal social relations. Thus it was the people with cross-cutting ties who initiated negotiations and pressed for compromise.

In terms of the *amount of compensation* to be given to the victim's group, there is usually some form of compromise made by the offending and the offended group. However, this compromise is not arbitrarily arrived at, but rather is an adjustment of an ideal standard of what the compromise should be, given the seriousness of the crime, the status of the victim, and several other variables. The following studies illustrate this process.

Kroeber's account of the Yurok Indians[13] makes it clear that among these northern California Indians, "it was well understood that 'every possession and privilege, and every injury and offense' could 'be exactly valued in terms of property'; and that 'every invasion of privilege and property must be exactly compensated.' "[14] Restitution took the form of various types of wealth and service, and the amount of restitution depended on the harm done to the victim rather than the economic status of the offender. In fact, it was the harm done to the victim plus the status of the victim that served to determine the amount of compensation in any given case.

For killing a man of social standing the indemnity was fifteen strings of dentalium, with perhaps red obsidian, and a woodpecker scalp headband, besides handing over a daughter. A common man was worth only ten strings of dentalium. A seduction followed by a pregnancy cost five strings of dentalium or twenty woodpecker scalps. . . .

In short, as Bohannon points out, "these Indians had a strong feeling for the definition of rights and obligations, and recognized certain appropriate damages for any private delicts."[15]

In Barton's study of the Ifugao,[16] Bohannon states:

An even more elaborate unwritten code of indemnity, with a sliding scale of payment depending on the social position of the injured party is recognized by the Ifugao of Northern Luzon. . . . These people, like the Yurok, are also without tribal organization, and settlement of claims is effected simply by means of negotiations between the parties. But among the Ifugao the negotiations are carried on not by the parties themselves but by a compromiser, or go-between, selected for the purpose by the parties. The go-between has no authority and no force behind him; there is nothing to support his efforts to secure a settlement by acting for both parties except the fact that the only alternative to settlement is a long-drawn-out feud, which is wanted by neither party and nobody else.[17]

In speaking about restitution for homicide, Barton notes the following pattern:

The rank of the slain has something to do with the amount of the labod [fine assessed for homicide]. The amounts given above are those that would be collected in the case of the killing of a Kiangan man of the *kadangyang* class. If the slain were a middle class or poor man, the amounts would not be so great. If the slayer were a middle class, or poor man, the amounts above might be lessened somewhat, but not very much. If the slayer be unable to pay, he is saddled with the rest as a debt. If he cannot pay the debt during his lifetime, his children must pay it.[18]

In the same work Barton also reminds us of similar practices of our Saxon forefathers.

Pospisil's study of the Kapauku[19] explains that among the Kapauku,

The amount of indemnity varies according to the damage done to the other party. It seldom varies with the status of the plaintiff. A rich defendant, however, may be charged a higher indemnity than an objective estimate of the damage would suggest.[20]

It is also important to note that the sanction of restitution was only one part of a much larger sanctioning system among the Kapauku, which consisted of corporal, psychological, and other economic sanctions according to Pospisil.

Among the Nuer, the Middle Atlas tribes, and the Egyptian Bedouin of the Sinai and Western Desert, again, it is the nature of the crime and the status of the victim that are the primary determinants of the amount of restitution to be given, not the economic status of the offender. Austin Kennett describes the process of restitution in cases involving killings, debts, and wounds.[21] He also depicts the general rules used in determining the proper amount of restitution. For instance, the restitution for wounds varied according to the following typology of wound inflicted.

Arab Law in Sinai, under the headings of Damages for Wounds, is divided into four distinct sections:

1. Loss of Limbs;
2. Broken bones;
3. Wounds on the face;
4. Wounds *not* on the face;

and a distinct code dealing with each of these headings is to be found.[22]

However, Kennett reminds us that there is a discrepancy between the presence of general rules and the use made of them.

The fact must not be lost sight of that the primary and fundamental idea at the back of all Bedouin Law is to make peace between the conflicting parties and to obviate the possibility of reprisals.
Hence "each case is legislated for separately."[23]

Much of the preceding data are in direct contradiction to Edelhertz's statements that:

The economic status of the offender influences the remedy imposed to a greater degree than does the harm to his victim ... the threat of punishment is traded off for dollars or equivalent services, with victims only incidental parties.[24]

The data are also relevant to Edelhertz's conclusion, noted by Galaway, that "in its historic connotation restitution was designed to benefit the offender rather than the victim."[25] This statement is contradicted by the preceding data which indicate that, at least in these cases, the amount of restitution was decided in consultation with and to the benefit of the victim and/or his kinsmen. Undoubtedly, it also benefited the offender and his family, but not in the way specified by Edelhertz. Galaway, again summarizing Edelhertz's conclusions, states,

Restitution, historically, became the mechanism whereby the offender and his kin group make amends to the victim and his kin group and thus avoid a more severe sanction which the victim's kin group could legitimately impose.[26]

The nature of restitution in the societies we have examined contradicts the presumed historical universality of this statement. In the first place, it is often questionable that the victim's kin group could impose any other sanction (legitimate or illegitimate), and even if they could impose another sanction (which was most often the resort to force), it is doubtful that the imposition of this sanction (which typically led to the feud) would benefit the victim and his family. Feuds were mutually destructive and thus the resort to restitution greatly benefited the victim and his family as well as the offender and his family and the society at large.

There are two more components of the restitution process that need to be noted:

4. *The decision on the part of the victim's group to accept or reject the offered restitution.* The alternative, as we have just noted, was usually that of resort to force, which in turn often led to the feud—an alternative which, from the standpoint of all concerned, had serious drawbacks, and which, not atypically, would eventually lead full circle back to negotiations.

5. *The actual giving of the restitution.* In the case of the Middle Atlas tribes and the Nuer (as well as many other cases where liability is collective), it is usually the group (usually kin based) of the offender that pays the compensation, and the group of the victim that receives the compensation. There are important ramifications for the reparation process in the fact that it is the *group* of the offender that pays the compensation and the *group* of the victim that receives the compensation. This fact means that it is in the interest of the group of the victim to have him accept and abide by the negotiated decision, avoiding attempts at further conflict with the offender and his group since this would cause the group to forfeit their rights to compensation, and would most likely draw them into a feud. This group can use a variety of informal sanctions in implementing these goals. It is also in their interests to keep the offender in line in the future. If the offender again breaks the rules of the game and brings his life in danger (or is actually killed), then the compensation the kinsmen paid has been naught. Furthermore, if the guilty kinsman should persist in violating the rules of the game, the group will be called on to pay further compensation. All this encourages the group to use whatever sanction available to keep their deviant kinsman in line. Again these kinsmen have a wide variety of flexible sanctions they can use to accomplish this purpose, and they can make the life of the offender very uncomfortable.

It should be noted that since his kinsmen are those who best know the offender, it is also they who can best appraise the offender's culpability and the likelihood that he will commit the same crime again. If, in the group's evaluation, the person is a bad lot, they may prefer to give him over to the victim's group to do with as they will, or even do away with him themselves to avoid further conflicts. Gellner notes this occurrence among the Middle Atlas tribes of Morocco:

The tribesmen ... distinguish two kinds of fratricide, good and bad. Bad fratricide is such as is held to have been unjustified by the acts or character of the killed brother, and it calls for the payment of blood-money by the killers to the wider group of which both they and the killed man are members. Good fratricide is the killing of a brother who is recognized to be a nuisance to his kin and to others, and through being a nuisance to others, he automatically is a nuisance to his kin, for they will have to "bail him out" by testifying, or by contributing to a fine, or by getting engaged in a feud. Informants remember cases of such "good" fratricide: men taken off into the woods by their own kin and killed.[27]

Purpose and Function of the Restitution Process in Traditional Small-scale Societies

By analyzing the ethnographic examples mentioned thus far, what can the analyst conclude about the function and purpose of these reparation systems? We submit the following ideal functions and purposes as important:

1. *Prevention.* One purpose of the reparation system is to avoid further, more serious conflicts, particularly to avoid the feud. Since through the restitution—the reparation—system, wrong has been in some sense righted, the balance or status quo has been restored, and more serious consequences have been avoided.
2. *Rehabilitation.* It is particularly important in small subsistence societies to provide mechanisms for reintegrating the offender back into society without too much stigmatization so that he can again become a useful participant in that society.
3. *Restitution.* Most simply put, this is a means of providing for the needs of the victim. Again there is a recognition that the offense against the victim needs in some way to be righted if the society is going to function effectively by maintaining a belief in its justice by the members of that society. This function is intimately related to the following one.
4. *The dramatic restatement of values.* In the process of reparation, the society is indicating the rules of the game, as well as the values to which it adheres. If the reparation process addresses the needs of the victim as well as those of the offender, the society is indicating its desire to achieve some kind of justice for all its members.

5. *Socialization.* By indicating the rules of the game, as well as by dramatically restating societal norms and values, the reparation system functions to educate the members of a society in terms of these rules, norms, and values. An internalization of this experience is a vital part of any social-control system.

6. *Regulation and deterrence.* As we mentioned earlier, a wide variety of flexible sanctions result from the reparation process in small-scale societies. Since the negotiation process is public, the sanctions of public opinion, ridicule, gossip, and ostracism are brought to bear on the participants. Also, in societies with collective responsibility, it is usually the group of the offender involved in the restitution payment, and the group of the victim involved in receiving that restitution. These groups can use a wide range of sanctions, available only to close associates of the offender and victim, to keep the disputants, particularly the offender, in line. This multiplicity of sanctions provides for regulation as well as deterrence.

Clearly, restitution has many functions in these societies, and restitution is one among many sanctions operating in the social-control system of such societies. It is also apparent that as this type of society is brought within a nationally based legal system, one of the strongest areas of conflict between local law and national law is the absence of restitution in national law. Results of the Berkeley Village Law Project illustrate that this conflict can be observed in countries as different culturally as Zambia, Sardinia, Mexico, and Lebanon. One of the clearest examples of the consequences of removing restitution as a possible sanction and/or means of settlement in the criminal law comes from Zambia and the work of R. Canter. Canter focuses on the Mungule tribe and the problem of cattle rustling. Prior to the imposition of state law, cattle-rustling cases were settled by restitution. With State law, people accused and convicted of cattle rustling were sent to jail. To make matters worse, jailing people did not decrease the incidence of cattle rustling. The Mungule measure the competence of the legal system by whether there is a decrease in recidivism, by which they would mean a decrease in cattle-rustling cases. Since they lost confidence in the State legal system, the consequences were "self-help" and rioting.[28]

Variation in Traditional Small-scale Societies

All societies have some form of collective and individual liability, for as we have noted, even in societies where collective responsibility plays a dominant role, collective liability is used sparingly and mainly functions in defining relations between groups; all cases, such as husband-wife quarrels, for example, do not require restitution. As we would expect then, in societies such as the Nuer where joint liability obtains when a murder takes place outside the kinship group, rarely does the same level of collective liability obtain in dealing with killings within the kinship group; the same people who usually pay the restitution would be the receivers as well in such cases. On the other hand, where individual liability is predominant such as among the Zapotec Indians of Mexico, there have been cases where the whole town pays collective compensation to the State for the killing of a nontownsman. In our own society, although individual liability operates for crimes such as killing, joint responsibility often operates in the corporate business field.

At times the predominance of collective liability has been linked with the form of kinship system. Cohen has demonstrated that the presence or absence of kinship groups such as clans or lineages does not automatically mean that joint liability is present although he agrees that such organizations are conducive in socializing adults in joint liability patterns. In his survey of the cross-cultural literature, he finds that clan societies are not automatically associated with collective responsibility and indeed contends that where collective responsibility is found, it is never found throughout the legal system but is usually restricted to one, two, or three kinds of criminal actions.[29]

There are a few general observations that can be made from the literature. Restitution is but one remedy among many remedies in a society. The same society that uses restitution as a strategy may also use retaliation (such as restrained killings), raids, property seizures, and fines. Often the range of possible procedures are seen on a scale from least to most likely to result in escalation of disputes. Restitution is often but not necessarily associated with the presence of a clan system. It can be used in societies where liability is collective and in those where liability is individual. Fines and compensation are by definition associated with the presence of centralized political authority. Restitution and/or damages can be found in both State or stateless societies. Third parties such as mediators or go-betweens are common facilitators of the restitution process, but sometimes the process is negotiated directly between two parties. We have found societies that do not have formalized political systems—such as the Yurok tribe in California, the Ifugao in the northern Luzon in the Philippines, or the Bedouin of the Western Desert—can have very sophisticated unwritten indemnity codes. Such substantive law can develop independent of legal procedures, courts, and complex tribal organization, or a society can have a formal court system and not use it. The Japanese system of restitution is almost entirely settled by extrajudicial agreements; the Japanese prefer extralegal decisions because they do not focus on the conflict, as with judicial decisions, but rather on the negotiating process.[30] The Tyroleans prefer to settle a car accident at the time and on the spot of the accident, rather than proceed legally through the courts.[31] In several societies it was noted that spatial distance increased the propensity of an aggrieved party to resort to retaliation rather than restitution.[32] Finally, it appears that restitution is used sparingly in most societies, most often in cases of murder, theft, debt, adultery, or property damage.

Let us move on to consider the process whereby the decision is made either to restitute or not to restitute. Among the Zapotec Indians of southern Mexico, the predominant pattern is individually allocated responsibility.[33] Most Zapotec villages have courts where cases are heard and where decisions are made using the principle of situational justice; the components of a particular case lead court participants to favor one decision over another. Usually a disputant reports a case to court officials whereupon the police are sent out to collect the other party (parties) to the case. There is a process of direct confrontation and "venting of spleen" in most cases. The head court official, the *presidenté*, listens trying to figure out which of a variety of strategies would best cool the case and satisfy justice. He sometimes asks the disputants what they would like as a settlement; other times he listens long enough to decide for himself. Once he states decision, there is a haggling process whereby the decision is either accepted and dealt with on the spot or rejected whereupon the case is appealed to the next level. The decision may be punitive (e.g., the defendant goes to jail), restitutive (damages are paid to the plaintiff), or compensatory (e.g., a fine is paid to the town treasury); the decision may also contain all these components.

Whether the judge decides on restitution or a fine is determined by what is to be accomplished in a case. Among the Zapotec, settlement and prevention are the tasks of the court, and even punishment is meted out with this in mind. When the Zapotec speak of prevention, they are usually referring to the danger of a case escalating, thereby causing division and strife in the village. In analyzing some cases recorded on film some years ago, Nader pointed to the kind of considerations observed in making the decision to restitute or fine which indicate the situational aspects of "making the balance" among the Zapotec:

The best way to "make the balance" in the *policia* case was to fine rather than ask for damage, which the defendants would have interpreted as adding insult to injury. The punitive fines go to the third party—the *presidenté's* office. In this same case the *presidenté* sought to re-establish a relative condition of peace between the litigants and at the same time to prevent escalation of the conflict to feud proportions. In the Chile case and the case of the little boy with fright, damages were the best way to restore the earlier conditions of peace. . . . In the case of the bossy wife, the *presidenté* thought that neither damages nor punitive fines would aid restoration of peace.[34]

In another case that a father had brought against his son, both punitive damages and fines were sought. In all the cases it was the individual offender who had to pay.

However, restitution and compensation are not always individually based in Zapotec society. For instance, there was the case of a band of thieves who stole from many villages. When the leader of the thieves was caught, the villagers wanted to kill him. When the State heard of the capture, State representatives were sent to collect the leader to try him in the State court. When the villagers announced that they were going to kill him, the State officials said that such action might be against State law; but it wasn't against village law, and the villagers proceeded to kill the leader by stoning him right in front of State officials. The State's response was punitive: either they would jail the *presidenté* of the town (as collectively representing the village) or, in lieu of such jailing, accept the payment of a large fine to the State. The village cooperated in collecting the fine. Although such cases are rare, they do happen and reflect the corporate make-up of these villages.

There are some patterns that override the use of situational justice and the desire for peace. Increasingly in these Zapotec towns, as they become bicultural as well as bilingual (Mexican-Zapotec), the decision or outcome of a case is likely to be a fine (offender compensation to the state) rather than damages (offender restituting the victim). Increasingly the plaintiff is the village and the outcome of such village-citizen cases is either fine or community services or both. If an offender has no money to pay a fine, then he donates his labor as community service. The offenders in these villages are often proud of the work they have done: building roads, the church, the municipal buildings, the schools, and later the clinic. Fines have taken over from damages as the towns have come to realize that their civic pride and self-interest can be enhanced by court outcomes that serve to enrich the town as an entity. The victim may receive damages, public shaming and confession and, in addition, may share in the offender's contribution to the town's wellbeing through the town's use of fines.

The factors that influence the type of outcome sought in decision making are varied. Duane Metzger who worked in Chiapas, Mexico, was interested in where and under what conditions restitutive versus penalizing sanctions were used. In comparing the outcomes of cases handled extrajudicially with those handled judicially, he found that in private extrajudicial settlement restitutive outcomes were more frequent in family cases, and penalizing outcomes were more frequent in nonfamily cases. In public court settlement, however, the reverse was true. The outcomes were penalizing in family cases and restitutive for nonfamily cases. He also found that restitutive solutions were used in conflicts involving property but not in conflicts involving persons.[35] These people, unlike the Zapotec, see goods as replaceable and amenable to assessment in money or in kind, whereas people in their view are unique and no amount of money can serve as the basis for a judicial decision on outcome. The Zapotec make no such distinction between person-property cases.

Koch found in his study of the Jalē of New Guinea, that the residence of the parties in conflict determines the strategy of the victim in retaliation and/or requests for restitution. This is a society that does not have an authority capable of adjudicating disputes.

Let us assume two cases where *A* and *B* are the principals in a dispute and *B* steals a pig from *C* in a retaliatory action against *A*. If all three parties belong to the same village, *C* tries to negotiate restitution from *B*. If, on the other hand, *A* and *C* belong to the same village and *B* to a different village, *C* demands restitution from A. A man follows the same strategy in his attempt to obtain the customary compensation from the abductor of his wife. He will demand a pig from the woman's agnates if they live in a neighboring ward and if a state of hostility with the abductor's village or an expected violent confrontation makes direct negotiations with the abductor a perilous endeavor.[36]

Koch also found that strategies of retaliation or reconciliation (e.g., by means of restitution) were at the local intraward level also dependent largely on residential proximity of the parties. If the residence of the parties in conflict was separate, there was more likelihood of retaliation and less of restitution or compensation. Social relationships between parties is a good part of what defines the pattern of legal liability in society, and among the Jalē social relationships are reflected in residential distance patterns. Similar observations have been made elsewhere in the literature about the part played by social proximity in assessing legal liability.[37]

It should also be pointed out that the decision to restitute is, in addition to other variables, often related to the decision to take a case to a formal body such as a court for settlement. As pointed out earlier, Kawashima points to the traditional preference that Japanese people have for extrajudicial, informal means of settling a controversy and illustrates that preference by noting that of the 372 accidents that one railroad had in 1960, not a single case was brought to court, and only one case was handled by an attorney. Apart from the traditional preference to settle extrajudicially, Kawashima points out that "monetary compensation awarded by the courts for damage due to personal injury or death in traffic accidents is usually extremely small."[38]

Devising and Implementing Restitution in the United States

It is a fact that the social, ecological, economic, and political context of most of the societies examined in this paper is widely divergent from that of twentieth-century Western postindustrial societies. Most of the societies referred to in this paper would be called small-scale, with most members of the societies being connected to other members by multiple ties of kinship, friendship, ritual group, work association, etc. These societies have traditional economic systems with a relatively simple technological base. Furthermore, it was often the kinship system that provided the main political organization for these peoples. Authorities typically did not have a monopoly on coercive force and so could not enforce unpopular decisions. Rather they relied on their skills of mediation and persuasion in trying to implement decisions.

Though these societies differ radically from our own, an examination of their reparation systems is useful in highlighting variables, options, and possibilities that we, because of a limited conceptual framework shaped by our own culture, might overlook.

The cross-cultural materials suggest that we are an odd society in the way we view offender and victim. For the anthropologist, it is an obvious question to ask, Why it is that our society has been more interested in the offender than in the victim? Is our interest in the offender related to the difference between what we say we are and what we are? We are a country where everybody, we say, is equal before the law. Yet our jails are full of the poor and downtrodden. It is clear from the evidence at hand that there are at least two legal systems operating in the United States—one for the upper-income groups, and the other for lower-income groups. Our jails are filled with poor people. The model may be one of internal colonialism. At any rate, the colonial model helps us understand why there has been so much interest in the incarcerated offender and until recently so little concern with the victim. Is it the guilt that accompanies the realization that the laws in our democracy do not apply equally, and is the disinterest in the victim related to the evolution of nation-state legal system whereby the plaintiff role is assumed by the State, a situation that undermines the position of the victim, once plaintiff? This is not to say that offenders should not be punished, but rather that our selective application of law along income lines sabotages the basis of respect for law and justice that is so necessary to prevention and/or rehabilitation by law.

Most actual and potential legal problems in this country are between people who do not know each other and never will. Our professionals have not yet faced this problem head-on—the problem of order in a faceless society. As critics of the legal system since the turn of the century have shown, there is a price tag on legal rights in this society: i.e., legal rights go to whoever can afford a lawyer. This is a central problem for victims.

In small-scale society, the victim is a key component throughout the reparation process. This factor is important from several angles, particularly from the standpoint of the dramatic restatement of values. When a society does nothing to compensate its members who have been innocent victims of crime, it is doubtful whether its members will preceive the society's social-control system as being a just one worthy of respect. That it is beneficial for a society's members to preceive their legal system as just seems to be especially critical from the viewpoint of socialization and internalization, two vital facets of any social-control process. No system can rely on "catching" and forcefully sanctioning all violators, and on instilling fear in all would-be violators.

Restitution in preliterate societies is just one of the many mechanisms used to sanction violators and resolve disputes. It is not a cure-all. In some societies, as we saw, it was used for patterned types of offenses such as homicide. In others it was used when it was thought that restitution would work to settle a dispute better than other alternatives. We should beware not to oversell restitution as another crime cure-all but instead attempt to devise experiments that would help us find out where it does work. We already have a system of restitution working in the civil area of American law. How well does it work, and in what situations and among what kinds of people? Is anything from the civil area applicable in the criminal?

Our society is a mixture of collective and individual responsibility. As Moore explains:

To be sure, the kind of collectivity which is collectively liable has changed very much from preindustrial society to industrial society, but collective economic liability is an extremely important feature of Western law. For example, if one thinks of personal injury and homicide as exclusively cases for individual liability in Western law, has one not forgotten the importance of insurance companies, business and government corporations, Workmen's Compensation, and public health and welfare agencies?[39]

What we are finding is a restitution relationship that is grossly unequal. Individuals are being made responsible to collective, corporate groups. It may work if called a "fine," but there is no reciprocity here when called "restitution." In devising restitution systems, we must be cognizant of this dual, i.e., collective and individual, nature. In planning restitution systems, we too often proceed as if restitution would be used only in cases involving a single offender and a single victim. In these cases mutual benefits are not difficult to envision. However, it may be corporations who make full use of restitution systems, with individuals being found principally on the paying end (as offender). If the victim, for example, collects from an insurance company, and that company then collects from the offender, we have individuals being made responsible to collective groups. If in turn we do not also have insurance companies restituting individuals when caught in illegal dealing, then our restitution system is grossly unequal, and it is doubtful that the cause of "reducing the crime rate" is in any way advanced by its implementation.

We need to be wary. At the turn of the century small-claims courts were devised to meet the needs of the "little guy." By the 1960s we found that these small-claims courts were being used mainly by business for debt collection. We could be devising a system for compensating victims, thinking of victims as individual citizens, and end up compensating victims that are not individual citizens at all, but large-scale organizations such as insurance companies. In this case the function of the restitution system may well be class control.

In societies where offenders belong to a single economic class, as for the most part of the United States, the burden of control may become economically intolerable. Restitution is seen as a way whereby the offender can contribute to his own rehabilitation, to the cost to the victim while at the same time allowing the continuance of what appears to be class control. When the victim is a member of the power class, as with the example of insurance company "victims," the control function is complete and efficient.

Offenders may object because restitution is serving the interests of the rich in a legal system where the criminal law or at least the implementation of the criminal law is income biased against the poor and indigent. Restitution may have either healthy or detrimental consequences for society and for the participants in the process in a pluralistic, stratified society.

If attempts to do something about crime in America are to be anything more than a WPA program for middle-class and middle-range professionals or public relations for politicians, we have to face the possibility that our ambivalence about offenders stems from our awareness of the discrepancies in equality before the law in a democracy. If we are going to have restitution, we at least have to formulate it within a vertical slice—up and down the income ladder. We are working on restitution programs solely affecting lower-income groups when more people are dying of known harmful drugs every year than the total number of homicide cases reported. Maybe it is the "least-worst" way to treat offenders, but it probably will not decrease the crime rate. We need a more holistic perspective on the question of crime throughout our society.

Any analysis of the crime problem that focuses on lower-income offenders to the exclusion of other kinds of offenders is diversionary at best. Ghettos in this country are illegal. They are the heart of the crime reported, but they are not the heart of crimes committed. Why have professionals decided to focus on one illegal actor rather than another? The workers of Hopewell, Virginia, poisoned by Kepone have no criminal and proportionately little civil remedy available to them. If building codes and other municipal laws were enforced, our slums would not be slums. What we are suggesting here is that many problems that are now coming to restitution might better be handled through prevention and that some problems not being handled through restitution might be handled by restitutive means. As we noted when commenting on the comparative literature, in all preliterate societies where restitution is used, it is used to handle the most serious disputes, not all the disputes that are made public.

By virtue of our bureaucratized society, problem solving in the United States has been piecemeal and patchy. Professionals are used as agents of change, but our professionals are trained to see, in a detailed way of course, only one part of the problem. Our problem solving then is not only patchy; it is skewed. As a result, change is often additive, and if responsive, mainly responsive to the needs of the bureaucratic part of the system. If we really intend to do something about offenders and victims in this society, present restitution "programs" must be set in a wider context with attention paid to vertical rather than horizontal slices of American society.

Notes

1. Ernest Gellner, *Saints of the Atlas* (Chicago: University of Chicago Press, 1969), p. 126.

2. Ibid., p. 136.

3. Ibid., p. 126.

4. Ibid., p. 126.

5. E.E. Evans-Pritchard, *The Nuer* (Oxford: Oxford University Press, 1940), pp. 150-151.

6. Elizabeth Colson, *Tradition and Conflict: The Problem of Order* (Chicago: Aldine, 1975).

7. Evans-Pritchard, *The Nuer*, pp. 150-177.

8. Elizabeth Colson, *The Plateau Tonga of Northern Rhodesia* (New York: Humanities Press, 1962), chap. 4.

9. R.F. Barton, "Procedure Among the Ifugao," in *Law and Warfare*, ed. Paul Bohannon (Garden City, N.J.: Natural History Press, 1967).

10. A.L. Kroeber, "Principles of Yurok Law," *Handbook of the Indians of California* (Washington, D.C.: Bureau of American Ethnology, Bulletin 78, 1925).

11. Colson, *The Plateau Tonga.*

12. Ibid.

13. Kroeber, "Principles of Yurok Law"; Paul Bohannon, *Law and Warfare* (Garden City, N.J.: Natural History Press, 1967), pp. 9-10.

14. Bohannon, *Law and Warfare.*

15. Ibid., pp. 9-10.

16. Barton, "Procedure Among the Ifugao."

17. Bohannon, *Law and Warfare.*

18. R.F. Barton, *Ifugao Law* (University of California Publications in American Archaeology and Ethnology 15, 1919), 75.

19. Leopold Pospisil, "The Attributes of Law," in Bohannon, *Law and Warfare.*

20. Ibid., p. 39.

21. A. Kennett, *Bedouin Justice: Law and Customs among the Egyptian Bedouin*, 2d. ed., (London: Frank Cass, 1925, 1968).

22. Ibid., p. 116.

23. Ibid., p. 116.

24. Herbert Edelhertz, "Legal and Operational Issues in the Implementation of Restitution Within the Criminal Justice System," in *Restitution in Criminal Justice*, ed. Joe Hudson (St. Paul, Minnesota Department of Corrections, 1976).

25. Burt Galaway, "Toward Rational Development of Restitution Programming" in Hudson, *Restitution in Criminal Justice.*

26. Ibid.

27. Gellner, *Saints of the Atlas*, pp. 116-117.

28. R. Canter, "Consequences of Legal Engineering: A Case from Zambia," paper presented at the 72nd Annual Meeting of the American Anthropological Association, New Orleans, November 1973.

29. Yehudi Cohen, *The Transition from Childhood to Adolescence* (Chicago: Aldine Publishing Company, 1964).

30. T. Kawashima, "Dispute Settlement in Japan," in *The Social Organization of Law*, eds. D. Bland and Mileski (New York: Seminar Press, 1973).

31. L. Pospisil, personal communication.

32. Klaus-Friedrich Koch, *War and Peace in Jalemo: The Management of Conflict in Highland New Guinea* (Cambridge: Harvard University Press, 1974); Evans-Pritchard, *The Nuer*; Gellner, *Saints of the Atlas*.

33. Laura Nader, *Talea and Jupquila: A Comparison of Zapotec Social Organization* (University of California Publications in Ethnology, 1964).

34. Laura Nader, "Styles in Court Procedure: To Make the Balance," in *Law in Culture and Society*, ed. Laura Nader (Chicago: Aldine Publishing Company, 1969).

35. Duane Metzger, "Conflict in Chulsanto: A Village In Chiapas," *Alpha Kappa Deltan* 30 (1960): 35-48.

36. Koch, *War and Peace in Jalemo*, p. 130.

37. Evans-Pritchard, *The Nuer*; P.P. Howell, *A Manual of Nuer Law* (London: Oxford University Press, 1954); M. Gluckman, *The Ideas in Barotse Jurisprudence* (New Haven, Conn.: Yale University Press, 1965); S.F. Moore, "Legal Liability and Evolutionary Interpretation: Some Aspects of Strict Liability, Self-Help, and Collective Responsibility," in *The Allocation of Responsibility*, ed. Max Gluckman (Manchester: Manchester University Press, 1972).

38. Kawashima, "Dispute Settlement in Japan."

39. Moore, "Legal Liability," pp. 93-94.

4

The Concept of Restitution: An Historical Overview

Bruce Jacob

Brief Historical Background of the Concept of Restitution

In primitive cultures the crime victim punished the offender through retaliation and revenge.[1] Gradually, with increasing social organization in the form of kin groups, clans, and tribes, private vengeance was replaced by vengeance regulated by the collective order. When an act was committed against a familial group or one of its members by an outsider, the entire group joined in the process of retaliation. This pattern of vengeance between kin groups is known as "blood revenge" or the "blood feud."[2] The fact that social control went into the hands of the kindred and not some severe or bloody revenge explains the use of the word "blood" in the term "blood feud."[3]

Though the blood feud was an expression of vengeance, it was by no means without regulations and rules.[4] In fact, certain rules of retaliation became recognized as customary and proper. One of the simplest and earliest rules was the *lex talionis*, first formulated in the Code of Hammurabi, under which the wronged party was entitled to exact "an eye for an eye, and a tooth for a tooth."[5]

Blood feuds caused endless trouble. An injury once committed would start a perpetual vendatta.[6] As primitive groups settled and became stable communities, they reached higher levels of economic development and began to possess a richer inventory of economic goods. The goods themselves came to be equated with physical or mental injury. Gradually, the harshness of the blood feud gave way to a compensation system. Unregulated revenge was slowly replaced by a negotiation system between the families of the offender and victim and indemnification to the victim through payment of goods or money. The process of negotiation and the payment to the victim has become known as the process of "composition."[7]

The transition or evolution from revenge to composition has apparently occurred in many primitive cultures or societies as they have settled down and become economically stable. As a striking example of this, in primitive areas of Arabia about one hundred years ago, blood vengeance was practiced among the nomadic tribes outside the towns while those living in the towns utilized the composition process as the means of redressing criminal wrongs to avoid the socially disintegrating effects of retaliation.[8] In one form or another the composition system prevails or has prevailed over a great part of the world—among the North American Indians, in the Malay Archipelago, in New Guinea, among the Indian hill tribes, among the tribes of the Caucasus, the Somali of East Africa, the Negroes of the West Coast of Africa, and others.[9]

As the community became structured and its leadership more centralized, codes of law were enacted to serve as guidelines for acceptable behavior. The laws of these societies contained monetary evaluations for offenses as compensation or composition to the victim.[10] Composition under such codes was used as a means of providing indemnification for the victim among the ancient Babylonians (under the Code of Hammurabi), the Hebrews (under Mosaic law), the ancient Greeks, the Romans, and the ancient Germans, and the English.[11] The law of Moses required fourfold restitution for stolen sheep, and fivefold for stolen oxen.[12] In ancient Roman, according to the Law of the Twelve Tables, a thief was obliged to pay double the value of the stolen property. In cases in which the stolen object was found in the course of a house search, he was to pay three times the value, or four times the value if he resisted the house search. He was to pay four times the value of the stolen object if he had taken it by robbery.[13] The Code of Hammurabi was notorious for its deterrent cruelty. In some cases under that Code, the compensation amount was as much as thirty times the value of the damage caused.[14] Under the Germanic laws, the amount of compensation varied not only according to the nature of the crime but also according to the age, rank, sex and prestige of the injured party: A freeborn man was worth more than a slave; a grown-up more than a child; a man more than a woman; and a person of rank more than a freeman.[15]

In England, under the composition system, the offender could "buy back the peace he had broken" by paying what was called "wer," which was payment for homicide, or "bot," which was payment for injuries other than death, to the victim or his kin according to a schedule of injury tariffs.[16] The laws in effect during the time of King Alfred provided that if a man knocked out the front teeth of another man, he was to pay him 8 shillings; if it was an eye tooth, 4 shillings; and, if a molar, 15 shillings.[17] By Alfred's time, about 870 A.D., private revenge by the victim was sanctioned by society only after the victim had demanded composition and his demand had been refused by the offender.[18] An offender who failed to provide composition to his victim was stigmatized as an "outlaw," and any member of the community could kill him with impunity.[19]

In England, the king and his lords or barons required that the offender pay not only "bot" or "wer" to the victim but a sum called "wite" to the lord or king as a commission for assistance in bringing about a reconciliation between the offender and victim and for protection against further retaliation by the victim and the victim's clan or tribe.[20] In the twelfth century as the central power in the community increased, its share increased, and the victim's share decreased greatly. The "wite" was increased until finally the king or overlord took the entire payment.[21] The victim's right to restitution at this time was replaced by what has become known as a fine, assessed by a tribunal against the offender.[22] The State, in the person of the king, came to be defined as the offended party in matters of criminal law, and as a result the State's right to punish and exact compensation from the victim superseded the victim's right to recover compensation.[23] The disappearance of the restitution concept and the complete shift to the State's control over the criminal law was apparently the result of a number of factors. One was the desire on the part of the king and his lords to exercise stronger control over the populace. Another was greed on the part of the feudal lords who sought to gain the victim's share of composition.[24] Undoubtedly, another reason was that the system of composition was extremely harsh on offenders who could not afford to pay their victims, for such offenders were outlawed or placed in slavery.[25]

This shift from a system providing restitution to the victim to one involving complete State control over the criminal law occurred in many countries in addition to England. Schafer has said that, in continental Europe, the injured party's right to restitution grew less and less, and, after the dividing of the Frankish Empire by the Treaty of Verdun, was gradually absorbed by the fine that went to the State.[26] The composition system surrendered only after a struggle. Even after the State had completely taken over the criminal law and the composition system had been officially abolished in Germany, there are records of victims who were not satisfied with public punishment and continued to claim personal indemnification as well.[27]

The ancient historical evolutionary process thus consisted of several stages: (1) private vengeance; (2) collective vengeance; (3) the process of negotiation and composition; (4) the adoption of codes containing preset compensation amounts to be awarded the victim in the composition process; (5) the gradual intervention of lords or rulers as mediators and payment to them of a percentage of the composition-compensation award; and (6) the complete take-over of the criminal justice process and the disappearance of restitution from the criminal law. In this evolutionary process, the central government became stronger. Familial groups were replaced by the sovereign as the central authority in matters of criminal law. During this proces the interests of the State gradually overshadowed and supplanted those of the victim. The connection between restitution and punishment was severed. Restitution to the victim came to play an insignificant role in the administration of the criminal law. The victim's rights and the concepts of composition and restitution were separated from the criminal law and instead became incorporated into the civil law of torts.[28]

In the Anglo-American legal system, there is a strict separation of criminal law from civil law. In the case of a crime that gives rise to both a criminal action by the State and a potential civil action by the victim, the two actions are kept completely separate. In theory, crime victims have for centuries had available to them the civil remedy of a tort action against persons who have wronged them through the commission of crime, under the Anglo-American system. In practice, however, this remedy has been of little value. The offender was often unknown; and where he was known, the victim often could not afford the expense, in terms of money and time, of bringing a tort action against the offender.[29] Perpetrators of crimes were typically poor or financially destitute,[30] and a judgment against such offenders was often uncollectible. For all these reasons the civil remedy was not a very effective means of obtaining restitution on the victim's behalf.

Instead of a separate civil proceeding, in some countries the criminal case and civil action were combined for purposes of procedural processing. In the German legal system, for example, there is a process termed the "adhesive" procedure, which developed in the sixteenth and seventeenth centuries under which the judge of the criminal case was allowed, in his discretion, to make a decision on the claim of the victim for restitution within the scope of the criminal proceeding. In the German system, the criminal trial predominates, and takes precedence over the hearing of the victim's claim. The victim's claim for restitution is, for convenience sake, heard at the same time as the criminal charge, but the two hearings are, in fact, independent of each other. This procedure is used in Germany and in a number of other countries today.[31]

Even in countries such as Germany, which have an adhesive procedure, the victim seldom receives full compensation for the harm done to him by the criminal. As Stephen Schafer has said, after making a comparative survey of the methods for providing restitution to victims now in effect in various countries of the world: "If one looks at the legal systems of different countries, one seeks in vain a country where a victim enjoys a certain expectation of full restitution for his injury."[32]

For many centuries, the disappearance of the restitution concept from criminal law has been criticized by philosophers and penologists. Sir Thomas More suggested in 1516 in his book *Utopia* that restitution should be made by offenders to their victims and that offenders should be required to labor on public works to raise money for such payments.[33] In the eighteenth century Jeremy Bentham took the position that, whenever possible, satisfaction should be provided by the offender as part of the penalty for the crime. He suggested that both restitution in money and restitution in kind be mandatory for property offenses. He identified the need for a public victim-compensation fund to assist victims of offenders who were not apprehended or convicted. He recognized that a State compensation system would have to be developed for victims of insolvent offenders.[34]

Bonneville de Marsengy, an eminent French jurist, criminologist, and reformer in 1847 proposed a compensation plan that would have combined elements of restitution and compensation according to whether the offender was apprehended. In his view, the victim's entitlement to restitution was part of the social contract, and he felt that society should rigorously impose the duty to provide restitution on the offender. He also said that "if there is no known culprit, society itself must assume the responsibility for reparation."[35]

At the International Prison Congress held in Stockholm in 1878, Sir George Arney, Chief Justice of New Zealand, and William Tallack, a British penal reformer, proposed that all nations return to the ancient concept that the criminal offender should be required to make restitution to his victim.[36] Raffaele Garofalo raised the issue at the International Penal Congress held in Rome in 1885,[37] and it received consideration at the International Penal Association Congress held in 1891 at which the following resolutions, among others, were adopted:

Modern law does not sufficiently consider the reparation due to injured parties. Prisoner's earnings in prison might be utilized for this end.[38]

At the Sixth International Penitentiary Congress, held at Brussels in 1900, the restitution issue was the subject of exhaustive discussion.[39] Professor Prins of the University of Brussels proposed that restitution to the victim should be taken into account as a condition of suspension of sentence or of conditional release after imprisonment.[40] Garofalo made a recommendation that was summarized as follows by the American delegate to the Brussels Congress in his subsequent report to the Congress of the United States:

In the case of prisoners having property, steps should be taken to secure it, and to prevent illegal transfers. As to insolvent offenders, other methods of constraint must be sought. The minimum term of imprisonment being sufficiently high, its execution should be suspended in the case of offenders who beyond the cost of the process have paid a sum fixed by the judge as reparation for the injured party, exception being made in the case of professional criminals and recidivists. The State Treasury would gain, since it would not only be spared the expense of supporting the prisoner, but would be reimbursed for all other expenses. The delinquent would be punished and the injured party reimbursed.

In the case of serious offenses in which imprisonment is deemed necessary, Garofalo would make parole after a certain time of imprisonment depend on the willingness of the prisoner to reimburse his victim from his earnings saved in prison.

He favors a public fund to assure reparation for those who cannot obtain it in any other manner.[41]

The members of the 1900 Brussels Congress were unable to agree on any specific proposal to require reparation or to apply prisoners' earnings to that end. Finally, they passed a resolution merely readopting a mild resolution of a previous prison congress urging procedure reforms to increase the power of the victim of crime to obtain compensation through civil remedies.[42] It has been said that the Brussels conclusion "effectively managed to bury the subject of victim compensation as a significant agenda topic at international penological gatherings from thenceforth to the present time."[43]

Developments Between 1900 and the 1950s

Enrico Ferri advocated in 1927 that as an element of the punishing process, the State should impose a strict obligation on the part of the offender to pay damages to the victim. He based this argument on the ground that society has a much greater interest in prosecuting a crime than does an individual victim, and noted that the necessity of bringing a private action for damages is a source of abuses and "demoralizing bargains between offenders and injured persons."[44]

As Garofalo, Prins, and others at the international penal conferences held between 1878 and 1900 had recognized, raising the wages of prison inmates would be an absolute necessity in any scheme to require restitution by incarcerated offenders to their victims. However, history teaches us that this would be a monumental accomplishment. At various times in the history of the United States, for example, during periods when private businesses had difficulty selling goods, they have exerted political influence to prevent prisons from engaging in enterprises seen as competitive.[45] During periods when unemployment was extensive, labor unions have sought to restrict the use of convict labor for the reasons that goods produced by prisoners might undercut prices and wages of free labor, and employment of prisoners might decrease the number of jobs available to free labor.[46] Laws were adopted, both at the federal level and in various states, during the Great Depression prohibiting the sale of convict-made goods.[47] As a result, prison industries are not nearly as extensive or as productive as they could be.[48] And for those inmates who are fortunate enough to be employed in paying industrial programs, wages are extremely low.[49]

Although restitution by prison inmates has been impossible because of the underproductivity of prison industries and low wages to inmates, restitution has become commonly used as a correctional device for nonincarcerated convicted defendants as a condition of probation. Probation is a fairly recent development. In the United States, the first statute dealing with probation was enacted in 1878. That law authorized the mayor of Boston to annually appoint a probation officer as a member of the police force. The first statute in this country authorizing courts to grant probation was passed in 1898 by the Vermont legislature. By 1915, 33 states had authorized probation for adult offenders; by 1957, all states had done so.[50] Restitution is often imposed as a condition of probation, or in connection with the use of the suspended sentence. It is used chiefly in cases involving property crimes. It is not uncommon for a large probation agency to supervise the collection of millions of dollars in restitution for crime victims each year.[51] The victim's civil remedy remains unaffected by the existence of the probation condition. If the victim obtains a judgment against the offender, payments made under the probation order can be used to offset the civil damages awarded.[52]

In addition to formal procedures providing for restitution to the crime victim, informal methods have evolved that achieve the same end. For example, one prevalent method used by a person who has committed theft, when arrested, is to suggest to the victim that the stolen property will be restored if the victim refuses to prosecute. Other types of prosecution are either never initiated or terminated after being instituted, as a consequence of an informal arrangement under which the criminal has agreed to make restitution.[53] Almost everywhere restitution, performed before sentence, is considered as a mitigating circumstance in the imposition of the sentence.[54]

Recent Developments Concerning Restitution

During the last two decades throughout the world an increased interest in legislation has developed to provide monetary indemnification to victims. This concern for the plight of victims is largely attributable to the writings of Margery Fry, an English penal reformer, who set forth her views in her book entitled *Arms of the Law*, in 1951, and in a newspaper article entitled "Justice for Victims," printed in the London Observer in 1957.[55] Ms. Fry thought that we have neglected too much the customs of our ancestors concerning restitution. She said that restitution to the victim would not only redress the injury, but it would have an educative value for the offender. Her writings clearly emphasized the rehabilitative potential of a restitution scheme,[56] and only secondarily considered the benefits of compensating the victim. However, due to the practical difficulties inherent in such an approach, she later became disenchanted with this idea and instead advocated that society should assume this obligation and compensate victims as a matter of social welfare policy.[57] The term "compensation" in this sense means payments made from a State-administered compensation fund to victims, whereas the term "restitution" means payment made by the criminal offender to his victim as indemnification for the harm caused by the crime.

In 1959 a White Paper entitled *Penal Practice in a Changing Society* was presented to the British Parliament. The paper stated:

The basis of early law was personal reparation by the offender to the victim, a concept of which modern criminal law has almost completely lost sight. The assumption that the claims of the victim are sufficiently satisfied if the offender is punished by society becomes less persuasive as society in its dealings with offenders increasingly emphasizes the reformative aspects of punishment. Indeed in the public mind the interests of the offender may not infrequently seem to be placed before those of the victim.

This is certainly not the correct emphasis. It may well be that our penal system would not only provide a more effective deterrent to crime, but would also find a greater moral value, if the concept of personal reparation to the victim were added to the concepts of deterrence by punishment and of reformation by training. It is also possible to hold that the redemptive value of punishment to the individual offender would be greater if it were made to include a realization of the injury he had done to his victim as well as to the order of society, and the need to make personal reparation for that injury.[58]

The committee that produced the preceding document emphasized that the concept of reparation or restitution could be successfully incorporated into modern correctional programs only if the convicted offender's earnings could be raised. The problem of achieving wages for prison inmates commensurate with those prevailing in the outside world will not be resolved, they indicated, "until society as a whole accepts that prisons do not work in an economic vacuum, and that prisoners are members of the working community, temporarily segregated, and not economic outcasts."[59] Furthermore, no solution could be reached, they said, "until the general level of productivity and efficiency of prison industry approximates much more closely to (sic) that of outside industry."[60]

The writings of Margery Fry and the interest created in Parliament during the 1950s has led to the adoption of a number of victim-compensation schemes, as opposed to restitution schemes. All the victim-indemnification plans adopted in recent years in New Zealand, Great Britain, the United States, Australia, and Canada have been designed primarily to provide "compensation" rather than "restitution." A compensation scheme places the emphasis on the victim, while a restitution plan would place emphasis on both the victim and the offender. Compensation payments are civil in character, whereas restitution is criminal and punitive. Compensation schemes reflect a societal responsibility for compensating injuries resulting from criminal acts. They are a method of spreading the losses resulting from criminal victimization. Ideally, the criminal would pay restitution to his victim, either directly or through an agency. But a larger proportion of criminal acts do not result in apprehension, let alone conviction, of the offender. Also, offenders, as a group, are one of the poorest segments of society and often would not be able to make restitution. Because of these factors, restitution plans are more difficult to implement as a practical matter, and as a result recent schemes for providing aid to victims are primarily compensation schemes.

One of the legal theories that has been advanced in support of proposals for legislation involving compensation by the State to victims is that the State has a duty to protect its citizens from crime and that if it fails to do so, it incurs an obligation to indemnify those who are victimized.[61] A second argument is that since the State imprisons offenders and thereby renders most of them unable to answer to their victims in terms of tort damages, the State should be responsible to such victims.[62] The third and most widely accepted reason for adoption of compensation schemes is that the State should aid unfortunate victims of crime as a matter of general welfare policy.[63]

The first of the recent compensation schemes was the New Zealand Criminal Injuries Compensation Act, which became effective in 1964.[64] It established an administrative tribunal that has power to hold hearings on claims for compensation and make awards. Compensation under the Act was limited to personal injuries resulting from certain crimes of violence. The government reserved to itself the right to collect from the offender after an award has been made to the victim.[65] In 1964 the British government introduced a nonstatutory scheme establishing an administrative board to assess and award compensation to victims.[66] Beginning in 1965 California has provided compensation to victims through an administrative procedure.[67] Under the California law, a person who has suffered pecuniary loss as a result of a crime of violence may obtain compensation to the extent that he or she is not indemnified from other sources. When an award is made, the state becomes subrogated to any right of action accruing to the claimant as a result of the crime for which the award was made. The act also contains the following unique provision that applies during the sentencing phase of the offender's trial:

Upon a person being convicted of a crime of violence committed in the State of California resulting in the injury or death of another person, if the court finds that the defendant has the present ability to pay a fine and finds that the economic impact of the fine upon the defendant's dependents will not cause such dependents to be dependent on public welfare the court shall, in addition to any other penalty, order the defendant to pay a fine commensurate with the offense committed, and with the probable economic impact upon the victim, but not to exceed ten thousand dollars ($10,000). The fine shall be deposited in the Indemnity Fund in the State Treasury, hereby continued in existence, and the proceeds of which shall be available for appropriation by the Legislature to indemnify persons filing claims pursuant to this article.[68]

Compensation schemes have also been established during the past few years in such jurisdictions as Alaska, Alberta, Georgia, Hawaii, Illinois, Louisiana, Manitoba, Maryland, Massachusetts, Nevada, New Brunswick, Newfoundland, New Jersey, New South Wales, New York, Northern Ireland, Ontario, Quebec, Queensland, Rhode Island, Saskatchewan, South Australia, Washington, and Western Australia.[69] Almost every year, new jurisdictions are added to the list of those that have adopted victim-compensation schemes.

These plans are based almost entirely on the compensation approach rather than on the basis that the offender himself should be made to pay for his crime. It is true that the California act contains the provisions that fines may be imposed against offenders who are able to pay and that such fines are to be contributed to a victim-indemnity fund and that several of the statutory-compensation schemes contain subrogation provisions; but in view of the economic status of most offenders, it is unlikely that the state or government will be any more successful in pursuing these remedies than private victims have been in the past in pursuing civil tort remedies against offenders.

Although Margery Fry had been discouraged in her attempts to promote interest in a scheme for providing restitution and had decided, instead, to work for the adoption of compensation schemes, other writers have continued to urge for the incorporation of the concept of restitution the criminal justice process. In 1965 Kathleen Smith, who had some experience as a British penal official, advocated the adoption of what she termed the "self-determinate sentence" as a means of compensating victims and rehabilitating offenders. Under her scheme, an offender's sentence would be set in terms of money owed instead of in terms of time as under present sentencing systems. The offender's earnings while in prison would be utilized to make restitution, and as payments were made, the sentence would be reduced. Thus the length of sentence an offender served would be determined primarily by the effort he himself made to pay restitution to his victim.[70]

Under her plan, the court would direct what part, if any, of the sentence could be paid from private funds and what part would have to be paid from earnings while in prison.[71] The value of stolen property voluntarily restored might be deducted from the amount owed under the sentence. However, such voluntary restoration would not operate to automatically discharge an offender because fines would also be levied in such cases.[72]

In cases involving an offender too aged or ill to work, the court would be free to impose a term of imprisonment instead of a sentence in monetary terms.[73] All other offenders would be required to work full time while in prison. They would join labor unions and would be paid full union rates.[74] From their weekly earnings an amount would be deducted as compensation for the victim. As soon as the entire sentence consisting of the entire amount of compensation and fine due was paid the offender would be discharged and released from further confinement.[75] Amounts would be deducted from wages in the following order or priority:

1. Money for prison board and lodging
2. National insurance contributions
3. Income tax withholdings
4. Pocket money (a limit would be placed on this amount)
5. Compulsory savings (the purpose of this would be to ensure that the offender had money on his eventual release from prison)
6. Contributions to compensation to the victim
7. Contributions to fine, if any, imposed by the sentencing court.[76]

Monies paid for compensation would be poured into the victim-compensation fund from which the victim would receive his compensation.[77]

The idea underlying the self-determinate sentence is that, since the length of time the offender would spend in prison would depend largely on his own efforts, he would be motivated to work and improve his wage-earnings capabilities and that the development of such attitudes would contribute to the rehabilitative process.[78]

Another of these writers who has suggested that the concept of restitution be incorporated into the correctional process is Albert Eglash. Eglash, a psychologist interested in corrections, suggested as long ago as 1958 that restitution, if properly used as a correctional technique, can be an effective rehabilitative device.[79] He said that, since restitution requires effort by the inmate, it could be especially effective as a means of rehabilitating the passive-complaint inmate who adapts well to institutional routine without becoming trained for freedom, initiative, and responsibility. Restitution as a constructive activity could contribute to an offender's self-esteem. Since restitution is offense related, it could redirect in a constructive manner those same conscious or unconscious thoughts, emotions, or conflicts that motivated the offense. Further, he believes that restitution could alleviate guilt and anxiety, which can otherwise precipitate further offenses. He makes particular reference to the use of restitution as a condition of probation and the rehabilitative benefits to be derived from this practice. Eglash is of the view that, although a convicted offender can be encouraged to participate in a restitutional program, the inmate himself should decide to engage in the program if it is to have rehabilitative value.[80] Restitution, in his view, ought not to be something done for the offender or to him. It requires effort on his part. Eglash aptly calls the type of restitution he advocates, "creative restitution."

Stephen Schafer, the author of several works on restitution by the offender to his victim, conducted a research study during the early 1960s among inmates in the Florida correctional system to determine their attitudes on the subject.[81] He surveyed inmates who had committed three types of offenses—criminal homicide, aggravated assault, and theft with violence. His study indicated that the overwhelming majority of those who had committed some form of criminal homicide wished that they could make some restitution. The author could detect no attitude, positive or negative, in most of the offenders in the other two categories. Schafer believes that the high percentage among criminal homicide offenders is at least partially due to the fact that many of those surveyed were soon to be executed for their crimes, and that their desire to make reparation might have been attributable to their proximity to death. In discussing the offenders sentenced for the other two types of offenses, Schafer said:

These offenders, at least many of them, did not appear to be intropunitive and thus could not accept their functional responsibility. Their understanding of incarceration seemed limited to what they viewed as merely a normative wrong that has to be paid to the agencies of criminal justice, but to no one else.[82]

It is Schafer's position that the offender should be made to recognize his responsibility to the injured victim and that this can be accomplished through the restitution process.[83]

Summary of Past History: Future Directions

The process of composition, which involved restitution to the victim, constituted a significant phase in the development of the criminal law. Restitution thus was an important concept in the history of criminal law.

Later in history, the State began to take more and more of the composition award and finally took over the criminal process entirely. The concept of restitution became separated from criminal law and instead became a branch of the civil law of torts. The tort remedy, however, did not provide a satisfactory solution to the problem of providing adequate redress to the crime victim. To a large extent, the victim has been forgotten. As a result, penologists have urged for many years that we should again utilize restitution as a correctional device.

In recent years there has been a reawakening of interest in crime victims. Schemes to compensate victims have developed in many jurisdictions. These have been compensation, rather than restitution, programs involving payment by the State to the victim. The offender is not involved in these schemes. Of course, subrogation claims by the State against offenders, to recoup amounts paid to victims, are possible under some of these plans, but such claims are rarely instituted.

During the past 75 years, the concept of restitution has become used increasingly as a condition of probation and suspended sentences. It is used in this way primarily in cases involving property crimes, and not in cases involving crimes against the person or crimes of violence. At present, restitution has not been used to any degree as a correctional method to deal with incarcerated convicted persons.

Should we be satisfied with the present stage of the development and use the concept of restitution, or should we seek to expand the use of the concept? In what ways will the concept of restitution be used in the future?

We can probably look forward to a continuing increase in the number of jurisdictions that will adopt statutory schemes for providing compensation to victims. It seems obvious that compensation schemes are necessary, but it is also true that the concepts of restitution and compensation are not mutually exclusive, and it is possible for them to exist side by side in a justice system. What is needed is a combination of both.

Undoubtedly, the courts will continue to utilize restitution more and more as a condition of probation and a condition attached to the suspended sentence. In the future, perhaps this use of restitution will be expanded to include cases involving crimes against the person and crimes of violence as well as crimes against property.

In the future should restitution be limited to cases involving offenders on probation and those under suspended sentences, or should it be expanded and used for other types of offenders, including those confined in penitentiaries? Expanding the use of restitution to include penitentiary inmates is an appealing idea, but an idea that is often criticized as being unrealistic and unworkable. It is clear that no large-scale plan to incorporate the element of reparation by the offender to the victim into current correctional practice would be likely to succeed unless earnings of prison inmates could be raised substantially. To raise wages, it would be necessary to add new prison industries and work programs and increase the size and productivity of those already in existence. This is probably not possible unless we take certain steps: (1) repeal or modify the present federal and state statutory limitation in the United States, which have for many years stifled the development of prison industries; (2) increase the market for prison-made or prison-grown goods and products; and (3) obtain the cooperation of labor organizations and private business and industry.

The first step has the support of the President's Commission on Law Enforcement and Administration of Justice, which recommended in 1967 that, "State and Federal Laws restricting the sale of prison-made products should be modified or repealed."[84] Should these restrictions be removed, prison products could be sold on the open market in competition with those produced by private enterprises.

Even under the present restrictions there are alternative means to increase the market for prison products. State prison systems are generally allowed to sell goods and products to public agencies or institutions, and Federal Prison Industries is allowed to sell its products to federal agencies. At present only a small fraction of the potential of the public market has been exploited. Federal Prison Industries could produce many items needed by other federal agencies which are currently purchased from private business. This proposal is equally applicable to state-prison industries and state agencies.

These proposals are likely to arouse varying degrees of opposition from business and organized labor. Governments should strive to cushion the economic impact on those businesses likely to be affected. Perhaps tax incentives or advantages, both state and federal, could be given to any private corporation willing to utilize prison labor or to establish an industrial plant or other enterprise at a prison. Utilization of skilled union members in overseer and instructional positions in these prison industries might serve to minimize union opposition.

Another method of enabling penitentiary inmates to raise money for the purpose of making restitution would be to place greater numbers in work-release programs. An inmate in such a program would be able to work at full civilian wages and thereby raise sufficient funds to make restitution to his victim.

If restitution is to be more extensively used, we will need to develop procedures to be used in determining the amount of restitution that should be made by each offender. Probably the easiest and most effective way to do this would be to allow the judge in the criminal case to make this decision. The criminal trial judge or jury would find the defendant guilty or not guilty. The judge would decide how much the convicted offender should pay as restitution for his crime. Also the court would set a term of imprisonment as the sentence for the offender as under the present system. The defendant would be allowed to appeal from the restitution decision of the court as well as from the judgment of conviction and the remainder of the sentence.

A number of factors should be considered by the criminal trial court in determining how much money the offender should owe as restitution for the crime. The basis for the determination could include medical bills for physical injuries or the value of property lost or destroyed. The criminal court should be free to make its own determination, even if in a separate administrative hearing compensation has already been awarded to the victim. The criminal court should be allowed to consider the physical pain and mental anguish suffered by the victim and loss of earning capacity, regardless of whether the tribunal making the compensation award is allowed to include these items. Arguably, the inclusion of these items may contribute to the rehabilitative process by making the offender more fully aware of the harm he has caused. Ultimately perhaps some sort of system for judging the harm done such as workmen's compensation schedules will have to be devised.

Another question that must be answered in any system of restitution is whether the offender should pay restitution directly to the victim, or instead into a general compensation fund. The ideal solution to this is that every nation or state should establish a victim-compensation fund. All restitution payments by offenders would be deposited in the compensation fund, and the legislature would probably have to contribute additional monies from time to time.

Each state should enact laws to provide compensation to victims of crime. Such legislation could be similar to one or more of the compensation plans already in existence. The compensation procedure and the combination criminal trial-restitution proceeding should be separate. The victim should receive compensation from the State regardless of whether the offender is apprehended or convicted. Compensation payments to victims would be determined by a specific administrative agency and paid directly from the fund.

How would the offender's sentence be reduced, if at all, as a result of compliance with the order requiring restitution in his case? From the prison inmate's earnings each week a certain percentage would be deducted and paid as reparation into the state victim-compensation fund. Also payments could be made from those earnings to the inmate's own family or dependents. Periodic statements would be given the inmate to show him how much of the total restitution owed to the victim has been paid at any given time. As the offender who has been "sentenced" to make restitution makes his payments, whether from earnings while on probation, prison earnings, or work-release earnings, the length of his sentence should be correspondingly reduced. The judge who sentenced him should have the power to reopen the case and reconsider and reduce the sentence. The court could be given complete discretionary power to thus reduce sentences, or its power could be based on a statutory table that would contain a sliding scale requiring that the sentence be reduced by a given percentage whenever the offender shows that he has paid a given number of dollars in restitution payments and the amount paid represents a given percentage of the total amount owed. The decision on whether to parole an inmate would be based, in large measure, on the effort he shows in making restitution payments while in prison. Also restitution could be made one of the conditions of continuing parole.

Many problems must be solved in incorporating the concept of restitution into the criminal-correctional process, but it seems clear that the results will be worth the effort. LeRoy Lamborn has said:

A renewed concern for a victim orientation in criminal theory does not mean a retreat from interest in the criminal; rather, the hope is that a substantial interest in the perspective of the victim will supplement the traditional criminal orientation and that the two together will increase the success of efforts to prevent crime, treat the criminal, and compensate the victim.[85]

Notes

1. Stephen Schafer, *The Victim and His Criminal* (New York: Random House, 1968), pp. 8, 10; Marvin Wolfgang, "Victim-Compensation in Crimes of Personal Violence," *Minnesota Law Review* 50 (1965): 223-224; Comment, "Compensation to Victims of Violent Crimes," *Northwestern University Law Review* 61 (1966): 76-78.

2. Schafer, *The Victim and His Criminal*, pp. 8, 10; Wolfgang, "Victim Compensation," p. 224.

3. Stephen Schafer, "The Victim and His Criminal-Victimology," U.S. President's Commission on Law Enforcement and Administration of Justice, Reference Documents (Washington, D.C.: U.S. Government Printing Office, 1968).

4. L.T. Hobhouse, "Law and Justice" in *Considering the Victim* eds. Joe Hudson and Burt Galaway (Springfield, Illinois: Thomas Press, 1976.

5. Ibid.

6. Stephen Schafer, *Compensation and Restitution to Victims of Crime* (Montclair: Patterson Smith, 1970).

7. Schafer, *The Victim and His Criminal*, pp. 5, 11, 14; Wolfgang, "Victim Compensation," p. 224.

8. Wolfgang, "Victim Compensation," p. 225.

9. Hobhouse, "Law and Justice," pp. 9, 10.

10. Richard E. Laster, "Criminal Restitution: A Survey of its Past History" in Hudson and Galaway, eds., *Considering the Victim*, p. 20.

11. Schafer, *The Victim and His Criminal*; Stephen Schafer, *Restitution to Victims of Crime* (Chicago: Quadrangle Books, 1960).

12. Schafer, *The Victim and His Criminal*, pp. 11-12.

13. Schafer, *Restitution to Victims of Crime*.

14. Schafer, *Compensation and Restitution to Victims of Crime*, p. 4.

15. Ibid., p. 6.

16. Hudson and Galaway, *Considering the Victim*, p. xix; Schafer, *Compensation and Restitution to Victims of Crime*, p. 7. Comment, "Compensation to Victims," pp. 78-79.

17. Schafer, *The Victim and His Criminal*, p. 16.

18. Comment, "Compensation to Victims," p. 78.

19. Schafer, *The Victim and His Criminal*, p. 17.

20. Ibid., p. 18; Comment, "Compensation to Victims," p. 78.

21. Schafer, *The Victim and His Criminal*, p. 19; Wolfgang, "Victim Compensation," p. 228.

22. Gilbert Geis, "State Compensation to Victims of Violent Crime," U.S. President's Commission on Law Enforcement and Administration of Justice, *Task Force Report: Crime and Its Impact—An Assessment* (Washington, D.C.: U.S. Government Printing Office, 1967), pp. 157-159.

23. Schafer, *Compensation and Restitution*, p. 6; Hudson and Galaway, *Considering the Victim*, p. xix.

24. Schafer, *Compensation and Restitution*, p. 8; Wolfgang, "Victim Compensation," p. 228; Comment, "Compensation to Victims," pp. 79-81.

25. Gilbert Geis, Comments at the International Symposium on Restitution, Minneapolis, Minnesota, November 10, 1975; Frederick Pollack and Frederic William Maitland, *The History of English Law* (Cambridge: University Press, 1898), p. 460.

26. Schafer, "The Victim and His Criminal-Victimology," p. 7.

27. Schafer, *Compensation and Restitution*, p. 9.

28. Hudson and Galaway, *Considering the Victim*, pp. xix, xxiv; Schafer, *Compensation and Restitution*, p. 7.

29. Wolfgang, "Victim Compensation," p. 223.

30. Home Office, *Compensation for Victims of Crimes of Violence*, Cmnd. No. 1406 (London, Her Majesty's Stationery Office, 1961), 2; Geis, "State Compensation," p. 159.

31. Schafer, *Compensation and Restitution*, pp. 6, 103.

32. Ibid., p. 117.

33. Thomas More, *Utopia* (J.C. Collins, 1904), pp. 23-24.

34. Hudson and Galaway, *Considering the Victim*, pp. 3-4.

35. Ibid., p. xx.

36. Geis, "State Compensation," p. 160.

37. Schafer, *The Victim and His Criminal*, p. 24.

38. Ibid., p. 114.

39. Ibid., p. 24.

40. Samual Barrows, *Report on the Sixth International Prison Congress*,

Brussels, 1900 (Washington, D.C.: U.S. Government Printing Office, 1903), pp. 25-26.

41. Ibid., pp. 23-24.

42. Ibid., p. 26.

43. Geis, "State Compensation," p. 160.

44. Comment, "Compensation to Victims," p. 72.

45. U.S. President's Commission on Law Enforcement and the Administration of Justice, *The Challenge of Crime in a Free Society* (Washington, D.C.: U.S. Government Printing Office, 1967), p. 175; Sanford Bates, *Prisons and Beyond* (Toronto: MacMillan, 1938), pp. 96-97.

46. Kathleen Smith, *A Cure for Crime* (London: Duckworth, 1965), p. 91; Mohler, "Convict Labor Policies," *Journal of Criminal Law, Criminology and Police Science* 15 (1925): 530-568.

47. Hawes-Cooper Act, 45 *Stat.* 1084 (1929); Ashurst-Summers Act, 49 *Stat.* 494 (1935); and 54 *Stat.* 1134 (1940); These acts are still in effect. See 18 *U.S.C.* § § 1761, 1762 (1964); 49 *U.S.C.* § *60 (1964).*

48. U.S. President's Commission on Law Enforcement and Administration of Justice, Task Force Report: Corrections (Washington, D.C.: U.S. Government Printing Office, 1967), p. 55.

49. Bruce Jacob, "Reparation or Restitution by the Criminal Offender to His Victim: Applicability of an Ancient Concept in the Modern Correctional Process," *Criminal Law, Criminology, and Police Science* 61 (1970): 152-160.

50. National Council on Crime and Delinquency, "Correction in the United States: A Survey for the President's Commission on Law Enforcement and Administration of Justice," *Crime and Delinquency* 13 (1967), 1-262.

51. U.S. President's Commission on Law Enforcement and Administration of Justice, *Task Force Report: Corrections*, p. 35.

52. Comment, "Judicial Review of Probation Conditions," *Columbia Law Review* 67 (1967): 181-183.

53. Wolfgang, "Victim Compensation," pp. 223, 229.

54. Schafer, *Compensation and Restitution*, p. 108.

55. Margery Fry, "Justice for Victims," *The Observer* (London), July 7, 1957.

56. Margery Fry, *Arms of the Law* (London: Victor Gollancz, 1951), p. 126.

57. Geis, "State Compensation," pp. 160-161.

58. Home Office, *Compensation for Victims*, pp. 4-5.

59. Home Office, *Penal Practice in a Changing Society*, Cmnd. No. 645 (London: Her Majesty's Stationery Office, 1959), 17; Geis, "State Compensation," p. 163.

60. Home Office, *Penal Practice*, p. 17.

61. James E. Culhane, "California Enacts Legislation to Aid Victims of Criminal Violence," *Stanford Law Review* 18 (1965): 266-272.

62. Ibid.

63. Home Office, *Compensation for Victims*, p. 7.

64. Geis, "State Compensation," p. 161.

65. Cameron, "Compensation for Victims of Crimes of Violence, The New Zealand Experiment," *Journal of Public Law* 12 (1963): 367-370; in 1972, New Zealand absorbed its crime victim-compensation scheme into a comprehensive program to provide reparation to all injured persons regardless of the cause of injury. Gilbert Geis and Herbert Edelhertz, "California's New Crime Victim Compensation Statute," *San Diego Law Review* 11 (1974): 880-881.

66. Schafer, *The Victim and His Criminal*, pp. 121-123.

67. *Cal. Govt. Code'* §§ 13959-69 (West Supp. 1975).

68. Ibid., § 13967.

69. Geis and Edelhertz, "California's New Crime Victim Compensation Statute," p. 881; Leroy Lamborn, "The Scope of Programs for Governmental Compensation of Victims of Crime," *University of Illinois Law Forum* 21 (1973): 21.

70. Smith, *A Cure for Crime*, p. 13.

71. Ibid., p. 14.

72. Ibid., p. 15.

73. Ibid., p. 24.

74. Ibid., p. 97.

75. Ibid., pp. 13-14.

76. Ibid., pp. 18-19.

77. Ibid., pp. 14-15.

78. Ibid., pp. 28, 37-38.

79. Albert Eglash, "Creative Restitution. Some Suggestions for Prison Rehabilitation Programs," 20 *American Journal of Correction* (November-December 1958), 20-34.

80. Ibid., p. 21.

81. Schafer, *The Victim and His Criminal*, pp. 82-83.

82. Ibid., p. 83.

83. Ibid., p. 127.

84. U.S. President's Commission on Law Enforcement and the Administration of Justice, *The Challenge of Crime*, p. 176.

85. Leroy Lamborn, "Toward a Victim Orientation in Criminal Theory," 22 *Rutgers Law Review* (1968): 733-735. Copyright Rutgers University. Reprinted with permission.

5 Legal and Operational Issues in the Implementation of Restitution Within the Criminal Justice System

Herbert Edelhertz

The offender who commits a crime is rarely so overcome with remorse that he feels impelled to make restitution to his victim of his own free choice. The criminal justice systems in which arrangements for restitution are compelled and administered differ widely in their objectives and in the degree of their commitments to achieving restitution goals. The economic status of the offender influences the remedy imposed to a greater degree than does the harm he caused to his victim. What we observe in both formal and informal restitution programs therefore are well-choreographed and one-sided bargaining transactions in which the threat of punishment is traded off for dollars or equivalent services, with victims as only incidental parties.

Since restitution transactions involve the denial or granting of liberty, the filing or nonfiling of criminal charges, the collection and disbursement of monies, and amendments to the conditions of bargains already struck, these programs raise a broad range of operational issues. Each of these operational issues in turn raises a number of thorny legal questions. These operational and legal questions should first be considered against the background of the relationship of the restitution remedy to specific program goals and the stages of the criminal justice system where restitution requirements are imposed.

The Relationship of the Restitution Remedy to Specific Program Goals

In setting up any restitution program, hard decisions have to be made as to the objective of the program, or some mix of objectives. It is usual that some emphasis will be given to the degree of victim harm or loss, but this factor is necessarily subordinated to offender-related considerations simply because of the limited capacity of most offenders to adequately atone to their victims in a material way. Victim interests can be better served by victim-compensation programs, which rely on State resources rather than those of offenders; further, such resources are not hamstrung by stringent problems of criminal proof.

If the interests of the victim are given priority in restitution programs, other

This paper is largely based on research made possible by Grant NI-99-0055, National Institute of Law Enforcement and Criminal Justice, LEAA.

program goals would become almost totally unattainable. Program emphasis would have to be put on squeezing every last penny out of the offender, regardless of the consequence to him and to his dependents. Pressures brought to bear could be so great that offenders could conceivably be motivated to commit further crimes to avoid penalties for their failure to meet restitution bargains.

Much of the current interest in restitution has been triggered by new developments in the field of victim compensation, and indeed there is often considerable confusion between these two types of programs. The political impetus for restitution programs is thus victim-oriented while the programs that are actually established invariably focus on correction or rehabilitation of offenders. No restitution program has come to my attention that had the delivery of benefits to victims as its primary or even very important operational goal. One practical result stemming from the offender orientation of these programs is that program evaluators instinctively bow to this fact of life by largely assessing outcomes in terms of correctional objectives rather than in terms of benefits to victims.

The Stages of the Criminal Justice System Where Restitution Requirements are Imposed

The first distinction that must be made is between private and officially administered restitution programs. We sometimes overlook the very substantial number of instances in which restitution is made without the offenses coming to public notice by an arrest or the filing of a charge. These situations are rarely addressed in considering the restitution issue because there is little any proposed restitution model can offer with respect to unreported crimes and also because these restitution transactions may well be unlawful in and of themselves.[1] When restitution is accepted by the victim as consideration for an expressed or implied promise not to file a complaint, it constitutes a compounding violation. Less questionable, of course, are instances in which restitution is offered by the offender (or his family) with the usually well-founded expectation that the victim will forbear to complain or less avidly cooperate with a prosecutor. These cases are often difficult to identify as compounding violations because of the carefully orchestrated semantics of negotiations by attorneys for victims and offenders and by surety companies.[2]

While there are potentially negative aspects to private restitution transactions, they do have the advantage of speed and the maintenance of goodwill between parties, as in cases of property damage done by children and costs associated with minor assaults. In many instances they probably serve to divert cases from the criminal justice system that should not be there in the first place.

Turning from the private to the public sector, there is another distinction to be made—that between informal and formal restitution proceedings, though the two are often interlinked. At the police level informal restitution is frequently standard procedure, particularly in the case of juveniles. Police will simply drop a matter once the victim is satisfied with being made whole by the offender. Another and more recent form of restitution is one in which police departments refer offenders who admit guilt to social agencies, which then "arbitrate" a restitution settlement between the victim and the alleged offender as part of formal restitution programs. While there are obvious advantages to such procedures, there are also real problems. In these situations, police exercise discretionary power of doubtful legality and without regard to their limitations of training and experience. There is also an obvious element of coercion in these cases, which may intimidate innocent persons to agree to make restitution rather than suffer arrest and the dangers of subsequent criminal proceedings.

Restitution may also take place informally, under the umbrella of what appear to be formal proceedings, after arrest and arraignment but prior to the filing of formal criminal charges. This is usually done with the prosecutor's knowledge and consent and is not, in theory if not in fact, a factor in prosecutors' decisions to exercise their discretion not to prosecute. In courts of limited jurisdiction, magistrates will often dismiss charges if the accused agrees to pay his victim for his medical bills or a day's lost wages. In some instances, of course, there may be diversion to formal restitution projects.

Restitution activity outside formally administered restitution programs frees courts and prosecutors for other important responsibilities, i.e., makes possible the implementation of priorities. Nevertheless, they may involve elements of discrimination that should be carefully considered for their legal implications and for subtle effects on achievement of broader offender-related program goals. Offenders who have assets (or who still retain some of the profits of their crimes), may have special leverage with respect to the exercise of discretion by police to refer, by prosecutors to charge or consent to dismissals, or by judges to dismiss.

Much of what has been said of the prefiling period applies to the postfiling stage—with restitution emerging as a consideration in the plea-bargaining process or in connection with dismissal of charges. After conviction, restitution is frequently a condition of probation.[3] Many states have made statutory provision for court-ordered restitution in conjunction with sentencing, and there is widespread statutory power to order restitution in juvenile courts.[4]

The restitution remedy can be implemented in conjunction with incarceration, for example, through allocation of prison wages to victims. Such programs raise a number of legal issues involving discrimination and coercion. Since prison wages are traditionally low, should higher wages be paid to prisoners making restitution? Would it be lawful to pay such prisoners higher wages than those paid to prisoners not saddled with a restitution burden? If the level of prison wages is raised for all prisoners, would it be fair or would it advance correctional objectives to allow higher net prison incomes (after deductions for restitution payments) to inmates who committed more serious offenses which did not lend themselves to the restitution process? These are only a few of the operational/ legal issues that could surface in a prison restitution program.[5]

At all the stages of restitution there are common operational/legal issues but little applicable program or research experience. Whether we are dealing with constitutional issues on the highest level or day-to-day field challenges, the same issues will confront program administrators. Which offenders are to benefit from or suffer from recruitment into such programs? What kinds of crimes should be considered compensable? To what degree is the amount of restitution to be tailored to victim loss or harm, or to offender's ability to pay? If a sentence includes a mix of restitution and incarceration, will it operate at cross-purposes? What legal and administrative provisions should be made for changes in the ability of the offender to meet his restitution obligation?

The Granting or Denial of Liberty

Central to restitution programs is the question of whether an offender can be deprived of his liberty or an equal opportunity for a probation sentence because he will not or cannot make restitution to his victim. The issue may arise in several forms and at numerous levels in the criminal justice process. In some instances the issue arises in a manner most difficult to assess, for example, when police or prosecutors exercise their discretion in situations where restitution alternatives are made available or where noncooperation with a restitution program may terminate the diversion process and result in referral of the offender to uncertain disposition by a juvenile court.

While the legal literature provides little reliable guidance for situations where restitution is compelled prior to conviction, issues of substantial due process under the fifth and fourteenth amendments to the U.S. Constitution are likely to be raised as diversionary programs increase in number and impact. The due-process clauses of these amendments promise offenders that they will not be deprived of their liberty in the absence of some rudimentary procedures such as hearings. Therefore the utmost care should be employed to make certain that no automatic or mechanical assumptions about guilt are made in diversionary programs that would saddle alleged offenders with the choice of acquiescing in procedures that imply guilt as an alternative to criminal prosecution or being labeled juvenile offenders.

The possibility of discrimination against those offenders who are unable to make restitution in perhaps compelling them to undertake menial tasks while others can buy their way out, can be expected to raise serious questions of equal protection of the laws and due process under the fourteenth amendment.[6] This issue arises whenever some public agency directly or indirectly establishes a class or category of persons and treats them more harshly than others without having a sufficient justification for doing so. While discriminations are permissible, they must be rational and not arbitrary; if unequal treatment is based on rational classification, states have wide discretion in this regard.[7] In the absence of racial classifications or violations of fundamental rights, courts will strain to uphold programs.[8]

These due-process and equal-protection issues are more likely to arise when restitution is required as a condition of probation or when probation is sought to be revoked for an offender's failure to meet his restitution obligation. Here, in contrast to the diversionary area, we finally find a more substantial body of law to guide us.

Judges have power granted by statute or they possess well-recognized inherent powers to discriminate between defendants in sentencing and in providing for conditions in conjunction with sentences. For example, Sec. 35.10, Subd. 2 of the New York Penal Law provides, with respect to conditions of probation and conditional discharges, that a sentencing judge may require a defendant to:

(f) Make restitution of the fruits of his offense or make reparation, in an amount he can afford to pay, for the loss or damage caused thereby. . . .

This is only one of many such state statutes dealing with adult and juvenile offenders.[9]

Similar powers are granted in a federal statute,[10] and the attitude of the federal courts toward this remedy can be illustrated by the words of the U.S. Court of Appeals for the *Fifth Circuit in U.S.* v. *Savage:*

Without question the court had the right to require as a condition of probation that the appellant make appropriate restitution or reparation to aggrieved parties for actual damages or loss caused by the offense for which he had been convicted. . . . Probation is conferred as a privilege and can not be demanded as a right.[11]

The thirteenth amendment to the U.S. Constitution that forbids involuntary servitude is not a bar since it makes specific exception for servitude "as punishment for crime"; and state constitutions have been similarly interpreted. In *Maurier* v. *State* the Georgia Court of Appeals also addressed the question of whether a restitution requirement constituted imprisonment for debt and said it did not:

That restitution to the injured party may be a condition imposed for suspending a sentence upon conviction of an offense . . . does not prevent the sentence from being valid and legal, and is not violative of the Constitution of 1945 . . . providing that [t]here shall be no imprisonment for debt. . . .[12]

Antipeonage cases would not appear to bar work assignments in lieu of money payments unless restitution programs are distorted into devices for obtaining and exploiting cheap labor.[13]

There has been speculation, based on two U.S. Supreme Court decisions that imprisonment for inability to make restitution would violate the equal-protection clause, but these decisions turned on the fact that the sentences imposed exceeded the statutory maximums, and in any event the offenders offered no evidence as to general treatment of offenders.[14] While the legal issue is not yet settled, policy as well as the legal considerations should be considered. Defendants should not be pressed to the wall or impoverished to effect restitution.

The National Commission on Reform of Federal Criminal Laws recommended federal legislation to provide that:

When restitution or reparation is a condition of the sentence, the court shall fix the amount thereof, *which shall not exceed the amount the defendant can or will be able to pay.* (emphasis supplied)[15]

And the same point was made by a New York court:

. . . if the suspension of the sentence is to be meaningful, the conditions of the defendant's probation must be such as are within the defendant's capacity to meet, in the light of his financial position and average earnings.[16]

The right of courts to order restitution as a condition of probation is clear. It also seems clear that this power to couple liberty with payment of symbolic or actual restitution extends to enforcement or collection procedures, for without reasonable enforcement mechanisms, this sentencing power would be meaningless. Without the power to jail a defaulting offender, enforcement of restitution orders would be almost impossible. It should be kept in mind, however, that conditioning liberty on dollars or labor carries us into areas where courts will be sensitive to possible arbitrary procedures, to treatments in which discriminations are not reasonably related to worthwhile program objectives, or to any other indications that our laws are not being equally applied.

Restitution Remedies

Restitution programs appear to be offender oriented; however, because their goals are almost entirely correctional, their scope and effectiveness are influenced strongly by the nature and scope of remedies available to benefit victims.

We have already noted that there are legal and policy factors that tend to limit the quantum of restitution to the ability of offenders to pay, but problems also flow from the fact that victim losses may be low in proportion to the gravity of the offense or are otherwise too easily satisfied. For example, one offense may be quite serious in comparison to another and yet result in only a small and easily paid victim loss. In the Minnesota Correction Center's program, the median victim damage was reported to be $139, and many restitution obligations were paid in short order; but the Minnesota Parole Board was unwilling to discharge program subjects from parole after completion of restitution obligations.[17]

The assessment of damages raises a number of questions that must be considered in restitution planning. There is a very real danger that the less the offense and the less the damage, the greater the burden that will fall on the offender. How can this happen? If we make the assumption that the more serious the offense, the more likely it is that there will be criminal prosecution or referral to a juvenile court, less serious matters are more likely to be the subject of diversionary proceedings. If the diversionary program is a restitution program, there is literally no limit to the restitution that can be compelled, and program authorities are quite free to take into account all offenses the offender is suspected to have committed. If the offender is criminally prosecuted, he has a number of ways to limit his restitution liability, unlike an offender diverted from the system. Most statutory restitution schemes permit restitution orders in connection with sentences only "for actual damages or loss for which conviction was had."[18] Therefore simply by going through the plea-bargaining process, a more culpable offender can lessen his restitution liability.

The Wisconsin Supreme Court took a different and unusually liberal view in *State* v. *Scherr*. It said that:

When a court in a criminal suit determines the amount of restitution for the purpose of probation, it does so as part of the criminal proceeding. Such proceeding determination is analogous in its nature to a pre-sentence investigation.[19]

However, in the same decision the Court declined to allow restitution for a victim's losses outside the time limits specified in the criminal charge, indicating that it was not about to permit sentencing courts to examine "a series of acts" that go very far beyond those for which a conviction is obtained.

Most formal and informal programs provide restitution only for actual damages, and not for common-law damages such as pain and suffering or permanent injuries. Where the victim has his damages taken care of through insurance or employment fringe benefits, a program that operates outside a statutory framework can order restitution to third parties such as insurers, but this may not be possible where restitution is a condition of probation. In a number of jurisdictions, courts have held that third parties may not recover.[20] It is difficult to justify noncoverage for such third parties if the primary goal of restitution programs is correction of the offender rather than responding to victim need.

The restitution remedy is in theory available to all victims who suffer damages. In fact, though, the remedy loses much of its practicality where the nature of the crime makes it likely that there will be a prison sentence rather than probation. It is not surprising therefore that with rare exceptions[21] the remedy has been applied mainly to property crimes and only rarely in the case of crimes of violence. For example, the Minnesota Restitution Center accepts only nonviolent offenders convicted of property crimes, and the Tucson Adult Diversion Program excludes all violent, sexual, or narcotics offenders. Of course, the restitution remedy can play a part in connection with parole following incarceration for a violent crime, but this also poses some problems. In a Maryland case involving a confessed rapist, it was reported that:

Watson will be eligible for parole in 15 years, but whenever he is released, said the judge, he must pay 40% of his income for the rest of his life to the two sons of the housewife he killed. [The husband said] the payments could only serve to remind his sons of their mother's murder, and might even put them in physical danger from Watson or his friends. [The husband] was going to be forced into the . . . position of hiring a lawyer to have the payment or reparations removed from the sentence of his wife's killer.[22]

At the present time there is no coherent or consistent operational or theoretical basis for answering questions involving who shall pay, how much shall be paid, who shall receive, and how much shall be received. Diversionary programs have little expertise in assessing damages. Courts have rarely applied their own experience in damage adjudication to the restitution area.[23] This is not surprising in view of the fact that the rationale of the restitution remedy is corrective rather than ameliorative. Greater attention to such issues as damage assessment is probably not a high priority because the obligation to pay is limited by the ability to pay, and payment itself is of lower priority than rehabilitation of the offender.

Administering Restitution Programs

Administration of the restitution remedy does not begin at the point when the restitution bargain is struck by a probation condition, an agency ruling, or a so-called negotiated contract of the kind employed in the Minnesota Program. Whether the restitution remedy will be invoked at all may depend on program resources and on administrative mechanisms available to meet program goals.

Since the aim of formal restitution programs—those in which specific agencies are set up for the purpose of administering programs of restitutive justice—is to correct and rehabilitate offenders, the existence of implementation mechanisms will largely determine which and how many cases are referred. For example, since most offenders have little resources and often lack marketable job skills,[24] developing jobs or subsidizing them may be crucial to the existence of a program and to continued referrals. Since this is an expensive measure, completion of the restitution obligation can also mean job loss for the offender—conveying a less-than-desirable message to a candidate for rehabilitation.

The nature of the bargain struck can be quite complex, involving not only obligations of the offender but also of the sentencing authority. In one New York case, *Feldman* v. *Reeves,*[25] the defendant had made his restitution payment in escrow, conditioned on his receiving a sentence of probation. When the court determined it could not do so, it ordered its Department of Probations to repay the offender.[25] While this case involved an unusual situation, it forcefully illustrates that the restitution bargain may be one sided or entered into by the offender under compulsion, but nevertheless courts will carefully consider what the offender is entitled to under his bargain. Simple and clearly described, bargain terms are therefore essential.

The restitution remedy is attractive because of its human appeal (the innocent victim has suffered damages) and because it does not yet carry the failure label which has attached to so many other correctional efforts. A juvenile or adult diverted into a restitution program may fail to meet his obligation and find himself referred back into the criminal justice system—this time with the added record of failure in a correctional effort—which can be expected to influence an ensuing exercise of prosecutive discretion. This raises the spectre that many offenders who would have been given a sentence of probation without a restitution condition under ordinary circumstances will find themselves in penitentiaries only because of this new and attractive remedy.

Because of these dangers, the collection mechanism must be carefully designed. Allowing direct payment from the offender to the victim puts an unfair burden on the victim. If the victim fails to notify the court or program of the offender default, it will weaken the correctional thrust of the effort, which relies and is centered on offender compliance with his restitution obligation. It is far better to have monies paid to courts or restitutive agencies and disbursed by them. Payments should be capable of being independently monitored, and timely measure should be taken in the event of default.

Where programs provide for symbolic restitution, e.g., labor in parks or other public or private facilities in lieu of cash, it is questionable whether private parties or officials of facilities benefiting from such symbolic restitution can be relied on to monitor the program. They may be unwilling to complain, thereby depriving a program of much of its planned correctional effectiveness.

Payment defaults should not be treated simply as enforcement matters. They may indicate recalcitrance on the part of offenders, but may also indicate the inappropriate nature of the original restitution bargain. Default hearings should therefore be an occasion to review the original restitution order as well as review of the narrow reasons for the defaults themselves.

Much attention has been given to the desirability of involving victims in direct contact with offenders in these programs. This course presents a host of administrative difficulties, e.g., do we penalize a victim who does not wish to cooperate? How do we protect victims? Elemental fairness should move us to avoid procedures that enlist victims by offering them rewards or calling on their sense of civic responsibility. They suffer enough without being selected to carry this additional burden.

In this brief overview it is possible to touch on only a few of the many administrative problems that may arise in the course of programs that have widely different objectives, procedures, resources, and offender or victim clients. We must keep in mind that formal programs have only rarely been carefully monitored or observed to date, and that the administrative problems of court programs still wait research attention.

Relationship to Other Remedies

Restitution programs do not operate in a vacuum. We have already noted that there are potential conflicts with other correctional programs and objectives and with victim interests and that these programs impact on prosecutive operations. Two closely related victim remedies warrant special attention, civil proceedings by victims against offenders and State compensation to victims of violent crime.

The existence of a restitutive justice program in no way limits the rights of a victim to pursue any civil remedy he may have against the offender. Because of the indigence of most criminal offenders, this is ordinarily not a profitable avenue; however, there may be cases where defendants are capable of making restitution.[26] It would be dangerous, however, to permit perversion of the restitution process for this purpose. The Wisconsin Supreme Court in *State* v. *Scherr* gave this warning:

Neither should the criminal process be used to supplement the civil suit or as a threat to coerce the payment of a civil liability and thus reduce the criminal court to a collection agency.[27]

Conversely, the restitution procedure should not be used to hinder or frustrate victim action. Offenders may try to hide behind restitution programs. In *People* v. *Stacy* the offender was ordered to pay $100 per month until $6,000 was paid. When the victim sued civilly for a far higher amount, the offender moved to stay the probation restitution order pending outcome of the civil suit. The court refused the stay on the ground that this would deter and inhibit the victim's right to pursue his own remedies.[28]

There is a close and important relationship between restitutive justice programs and victim-compensation programs. Table 5-1 compares the two types of programs. It should be noted that victim-compensation programs have substantial experience in damage assessment that should be tapped by restitutive justice programs. Future expansion of both types of programs could open the way to use of this experience by restitutive justice programs or even to assumption of the assessment task by victim-compensation programs on a cost-reimbursible basis.

Table 5-1

Comparison of Remedy Limitations in Victim Compensation and Restitution Programs on Selected Variables

Limiting Variable	Victim Compensation Remedy	Restitution Remedy
Requirement of offender apprehension	Not necessary	Necessary
Presence of benefit limits	Generally true	Rarely true
Victim eligibility requirements	Generally only victims of violent crimes	Theoretically, no limitations by type of crime
Financial need of victim	Sometimes necessary	Not necessary
Determination of offender financial ability	Not important	Very important
Presence of offender-victim family relationship	Prohibits receiving benefits	No bar to benefits
Concern for offender rehabilitation	Irrelevant	Extremely relevant

Most State victim-compensation programs are empowered to civilly sue offenders to recover awards paid to victims. These subrogation powers have thus far not been exercised to any noticeable extent. If restitutive justice programs should proliferate and operate effectively to recover damages from offenders, we may anticipate that victim-compensation administrators will seek to make recovery of part of their costs from offenders. Those who plan restitutive justice programs should take this program relationship into account.

Conclusion

Restitutive justice is but one way of addressing correctional challenges and but one way of making victims whole. It should not be given an automatic plus sign because it is a relatively unresearched field. The concept and programs developed to implement the concept should be scrutinized, evaluated, and compared with other ways of correcting offenders and helping victims. Since little is known, experiments should be encouraged so that we can learn more and develop fair and effective models for implementation.

Demonstration programs should be designed to facilitate evaluation. Cost-benefit analyses (addressing social as well as dollar costs) are vital to determining whether restitutive justice is a worthwhile correctional route. If it is, careful evaluations incorporating cost-benefit analyses should help us to determine which elements of restitutive justice programs should be given major emphasis.

Notwithstanding the very slim data we possess in this area, there is reason to be optimistic that fair, efficient, and effective restitutive justice programs can be designed to withstand the tests of well-designed evaluations and cost-benefit analyses. There is reason to believe that restitution and victim-compensation programs complement each other and can enhance the benefits of both.

Restitution programs should be simple and easily understood. They should address their correctional objectives, mainly by stress on completion of carefully described restitution obligations, and should avoid mixtures of restitutive justice and more traditional methods of offender treatment. Finally, if restitution programs are to be effective and have credibility with offenders, successful completion of the restitution bargain should be the final termination of individual correctional efforts, and not the end of one stage preliminary to referral elsewhere for additional correctional treatment.

Notes

1. Herbert Edelhertz and Gilbert Geis, *Public Compensation to Victims of Crime* (New York: Praeger Publishers, Inc., 1974), pp. 20-21.

2. Note, "Compounding Crimes: Time for Enforcement," *Hastings Law Journal* 27 (September 1975); Richard E. Laster, "Criminal Restitution: A Survey of Its Past History and an Analysis of Its Present Usefulness," *University of Richmond Law Review* 5 (Fall 1970): 83.

3. See 18 U.S.C. 3651 and *Study Draft of New Federal Criminal Code*, the National Commission on Reform of Federal Criminal Laws (Washington, D.C.: U.S. Government Printing Office, 1970), Sec. 3103(2) (e).

4. Among the states that have such statutes are New York, Georgia, California, Illinois, Wisconsin, Pennsylvania, Massachusetts, and the District of Columbia. Juvenile statutes are cited in Mark Levin and Rosemary Sarri, *Juvenile Delinquency: A Study of Juvenile Codes in the U.S.* (Ann Arbor: University of Michigan Press, 1974), p. 54.

5. South Carolina Department of Corrections, *The Correctional Industries Feasibility Study Market Research Phase: A Summary of Conclusions and Recommendations* (South Carolina Department of Corrections, 1974), p. 7.

6. Edelhertz and Geis, *Public Compensation*, p. 290.

7. Herbert Edelhertz et al., *Restitutive Justice: A General Survey and Analysis* (Seattle: Law and Justice Study Centers, January 1975), pp. 35-36.

8. Ibid.

9. Levin and Sarri, *Juvenile Delinquency.*

11. 440 F.2d 1237 (5th Cir., 1971).

12. 144 S.E.12, 112 Ga. Appl. 297 (Ct. of Appeals, 1965).

13. *Bailey v. Alabama*, 219 U.S. 219 (1911); *Taylor v. Georgia*, 315 U.S. 25 (1942); *Pollack v. Williams*, 322 U.S. 4 (1944).

14. *Williams v. Illinois*, 399 U.S. 235 (1970); *Tate v. Short*, 401 U.S. 395 (1971).

15. Study Draft of New Federal Criminal Code, footnote 6 *supra*, Sec. 3103 (2), (e).

16. *People v. Marx*, 19 A.D. 2nd 577 (Supr. Ct., App. Div., 4th Dept., 1963).

17. Burt Galaway and Joe Hudson, "Issues in the Correctional Implementation of Restitution to Victims of Crime," in *Considering the Victim: Readings in Restitution and Victim Compensation*, eds. Joe Hudson and Burt Galaway (Springfield, Illinois: Thomas Press, 1975), p. 355; Kathleen J. Smith, *A Cure for Crime: The Case for the Self-Determinate Sentence* (London, Cox & Wyman, Ltd., 1965), pp. 48-49.

18. See 18 U.S.C. 3651.

19. 9 Wisc. 418, 101 N.W. 2d 77.

20. *People v. Graco*, 204 N.Y.S. 2d 744 (Oneida County Court, 1960).

21. In *People v. Stacy*, 64 Ill. App. 2d 157, 212 N.E. 2d 286 (App. Ct. of Ill., 1965), restitution was ordered following a conviction for attempted murder.

22. *Time* Magazine, May 8, 1972, p. 61.

23. In *People v. Scherr,* op. cit., *supra* note 19, the trial court appointed a referee to assist it in assessing damages, a procedure criticized by the Wisconsin Supreme Court when the case came up on appeal.

24. Galaway and Hudson, "Issues in the Correctional Implementation of Restitution to Victims of Crime," p. 357.

25. *Feldman v. Reeves*, 356 N.Y.S. 2d 627 (App. Div. 1974).

26. See *Feldman v. Reeves*, Ibid., and *People v. Alexander*, 6 Cal. Rptr. 31.

27. *People v. Scherr*, op. cit., *supra* note 19.

28. See footnote 25, *supra*. People v. Stacy, *op. cit.,* supra *note 21*.

6

Toward the Rational
Development of Restitution

Burt Galaway

During the past ten years an exciting variety of programs have been developed to demonstrate the use of restitution as a requirement placed on the offender in total or partial response to the criminal or delinquent act. Restitution has apparently always been widely used informally both as a condition of diversion and as a court-imposed condition of probation. What recently developed programs have been attempting to demonstrate is that restitution can be used in a planned, systematic manner to accomplish some other end such as rehabilitation or correction of the offender.

Examples of such planned restitution programs include the Community Services program in England; Minnesota Restitution Center; the Victim Assistance Programs in the juvenile courts of St. Louis, Missouri, and Pennington County (Rapid City) South Dakota; the Restitution Shelters developed by the Department of Offender Rehabilitation in Georgia; the Probation in Restitution Experiment of the Polk County (Des Moines) Iowa Court Services; the Pilot Alberta Restitution Center in Calgary, Alberta; the Adult Diversion Project of the Pima County Attorney's Office, Tuscon, Arizona; and others. Some of these programs are serving as models for others. The Victim Assistance Program of the Pennington County South Dakota juvenile court, for example, was modeled largely after a similar program in St. Louis, Missouri, and has itself become the model for a program in Oklahoma. The programs in Georgia, Iowa, and Alberta were influenced by the experiences of the Minnesota Restitution Center. Quarterly reports of some programs report frequent inquiries by other agencies interested in restitution programming; one of the goals of the Minnesota Restitution Center is to disseminate information and to assist other agencies in their development of restitution programs.

Interest exists in expanding the systematic application of restitution in the correction system, and a group of program staff would appear to exist with an experience base and commitment to assist with such expansion. However, the interest and stimulus for expansion of restitution programming is, as is frequently the practice in corrections, considerably in advance of assimilation, analysis, and dissemination of information concerning the extent to which existing programs are attaining criminal justice goals. Further, most of the present projects, in spite of their exciting nature, have inadequate plans for either evaluation of outcomes or systematic recording and dissemination of data concerning program processes. Even in the projects whose original plan, frequently developed as a grant application, specified an evaluation design, these designs have either not been implemented or the implementation has been incomplete and inadequate. Thus not only is the impetus for restitution programming advancing faster than assimilation of the experiences of current programs, but these experiences are going to be of a reduced helpfulness in planning because of the failure to require adequate information keeping and evaluation or, if required, the failure of funding bodies to monitor projects to assure adherence to commitments to evaluation contained in the grant application.

The experience of restitution programs to date is helpful, however, in identifying what can be done as well as in suggesting questions for resolution. The experiences indicate that the following are possible:

1. Restitution programs can be established by a variety of criminal justice agencies. At present restitution programs are administered by prosecutors, private organizations, neighborhood citizen groups, juvenile courts, adult court services, and state departments of corrections. Furthermore, program examples can be found at all stages of the criminal justice process—pretrial diversion, prosecution, probation, and institutional services. Programs have been established which both distribute the restitution programming among existing staff and which specialize these functions in special units or organizations.

2. Restitution can be added to existing sanctions. The typical pattern has been to add restitution requirements to other sanctions or required services. Examples include adding restitution to usual probation conditions, requiring the offender to reside in a restricted setting while making restitution, and requiring the offender to participate in group counseling or other treatment activities while implementing a restitution plan.

3. Problems in determining the form and amount of restitution are resolvable. Further, restitution agreements can be developed under circumstances of direct victim-offender negotiations or circumstances in which the negotiations are through a third party without direct victim-offender contact.

The experience of successfully establishing restitution programs in a variety of criminal justice settings coupled with the growing interest in restitution programming will likely result in the continued development of a variety of restitution programs. Hopefully, expansion will include a systematic effort to evaluate the outcomes of restitution programming along with a careful analysis of some of the problems and issues that must be resolved as restitution is integrated into criminal justice programs. The purpose of this paper is to suggest three ways in which criminal justice planners and administrators can contribute to the orderly development of restitution in criminal justice agencies. The three methods are:

1. Careful analysis, assimilation, and dissemination of information from present restitution projects.

2. Creation of conditions that permit controlled experimentation with the use of restitution.
3. Development of descriptive accounts of alternative resolutions to key questions in the utilization of restitution.

Dissemination of Information

The first method, synthesis and dissemination of information concerning present restitution experiences, will be considered only briefly because it is largely beyond the ability of either existing restitution programs or agencies which may be considering implementing restitution programming. However a careful review and analysis of the experience of existing restitution programs would provide useful guidelines to agencies considering implementing restitution programs and avoid the necessity of continually reinventing the wheel. Useful information might be shared about types of offenders for whom restitution is used as a sanction, how restitution is operationalized, experiences with victims, reaction of the community to restitution programming, impact of the host agency on the restitution program, types of problems encountered and the manner resolved, and any available indication of the effectiveness of restitution in meeting program goals. Such a synthesis could, of course, highlight contrasts among various programs and suggest alternative ways of pursuing restitution programming.

For correctional planners such a cross program comparison and synthesis might suggest very useful clues in determining agency receptivity to restitution programming and, secondly, suggest possible variables within these host agencies which will impact and influence the direction of restitution programming. For example, from its inception the Minnesota Restitution Center required offenders to engage in mandatory group counseling as well as completing restitution commitments. To what extent did the group counseling requirement result from locating the restitution center in a host agency with a high proportion of treatment professionals in leadership positions and a strong commitment to group treatment approaches? This might be contrasted with the Georgia experience in which residents live in restitution shelters but are not required to engage in treatment activities while completing their restitution obligations.

While planners and administrators who are considering establishing restitution programs would gain from a synthesis of information about existing programs, the preparation of this material is beyond the reasonable ability of any specific program. But what *can be* expected of individual restitution programs? Two things can be reasonably expected. First, movement can be away from exploration in the use of restitution and toward the development of reasonably controlled restitution experiments. Secondly, good descriptive accounts should be developed about the way in which key questions in the use of restitution are resolved and the results which are thought to flow from the particular resolution.

Toward Controlled Restitution Experiments

If present restitution projects are viewed as exploratory, the next logical step is to build upon these experiences through the development of controlled experiments designed to test the impact of restitution programming. Movement in this direction will require the development of operational definitions of restitution. The formulation of explicit purposes for restitution programming, the definition of a population of offenders for whom restitution is considered appropriate, a willingness to use restitution as the sole sanction for a portion of the specified populations, and the development of research designs that permit comparisons of restitution programming vis-à-vis other types of criminal justice sanctions.

Operationalizing Restitution

A cursory examination of existing programs reveals that the term *restitution* is used to refer to a number of different phenomena. The term has been applied to a process in which the offender makes a cash payment directly to the victim, the offender makes a cash payment to a third party who forwards the payment to the victim, the offender engages in some sort of community service, the offender makes a cash payment to a community organization, or the offender provides a personal service to the victim. Sometimes adjectives are added: *monetary* restitution, *symbolic* restitution, *personal-service* restitution, *community-service* restitution, and so on. An immediate need is the development of a conceptual framework that clearly specifies and defines differing types of restitution.

A simple typology of restitution as illustrated in Table 6-1 can be developed by using two variables: whether the offender makes restitution in money or service and whether the recipient of the restitution can then be identified:

Type I: *Monetary-victim* restitution refers to payment of money by the offender to the actual victim of the crime. This is probably the most common definition and actual use of restitution.

Table 6-1
Typology of Restitution

		Recipient of Restitution	
		Victim	*Community Organization*
Form of Restitution	*Monetary*	Type I Monetary-Victim	Type II Monetary-Community
	Service	Type III Service-Victim	Type IV Service-Community

Type II: *Monetary-community* restitution involves the payment of money by the offender to some substitute victim. The Minnesota Restitution Center has been making use of this type of restitution as a direct service-restitution requirement became less acceptable to the parole board. This is also a corrective measure used by West German courts for juvenile and young adult offenders who can be ordered to make monetary payments to useful public establishments.

Type III: *Service-victim* restitution requires the offender to perform a useful service for the actual victim of crime. Existing restitution projects and the available literature do not provide good examples of this type of restitution although the Citizen Dispute Settlement Programs of the American Arbitration Association[1] and the Night Prosecutor Program in Ohio[2] are likely sources. Both of these programs are designed to bring offenders and victims together to effect a noncriminal settlement of private criminal complaints. The Victim Assistance programs of the juvenile courts in St. Louis and Rapid City, South Dakota, make reference to personal service restitution which appears to be of this type.[3]

Type IV: *Service-community* restitution requires the offender to perform some useful community service. Probation conditions requiring community service, the English program of substituting community service for imprisonment,[4] and the use of "symbolic" restitution in the first two years of operation of the Minnesota Restitution Center are all examples of this form of restitution.

Any typology of restitution will become more complex as additional variables such as victim-offender contacts or victim participation in developing the restitution plan are considered. Although difficult to assess in corrections, the issue of whether or not restitution is undertaken voluntarily or is coerced may be an important variable in a restitution typology. The Minnesota Restitution Center, for example, has developed restitution agreements calling for moral restitution in which the offender agrees to make restitution for offenses (such as checks) for which, because of plea bargaining or for other reasons, he was not actually found guilty. The restitution agreements containing such a provision have clearly specified that this was strictly a moral obligation and that failure on the part of the offender to complete the obligation cannot be used as grounds for parole revocation.

The limited experience with restitution to date indicates that the concept is broad and requires some refinement in order to specify differing kinds of restitution requirements. A present need is to begin defining these different types of restitution, identifying the factors that are characteristic of each type, and developing a useful classification scheme.

The typology of restitution here may or may not be useful in planning new programs. The issue, however, is to clearly define the nature of restitution to be utilized in a program. Factors that go into that definition—form of restitution, recipient of restitution, extent of victim involvement, extent of coercion, and so on, are, at this point in the development of the concept, less important than their clear specification. What is needed is the systematic demonstration of various kinds of restitution programs. Studies of a wide variety of experiences with different types of restitution (each individual type clearly operationalized) will, over time, provide clues as to what type of restitution works best in specified circumstances. To have an idea of the meaning of "works,"[4] the restitution program must have a clear purpose.

Purpose of Restitution

There is considerable lack of clarity about the purpose of restitution. Restitution has been advanced both as a program to help crime victims and as a program which is rehabilitative for offenders. Who are the expected beneficiaries of a restitution program—victims, offenders, community at large, criminal justice system? Promoting restitution as a program to help crime victims is popular but questionable. The vast majority of crimes go unsolved, many of those that are solved through the arrest of an offender do not result in conviction, and for many offenders for whom convictions are secured, restitution may not be considered an appropriate sanction. Thus a comparatively small number of crime victims will ever receive redress as a result of restitution programs. If the primary social objective is protecting the welfare of crime victims, then other programs— such as public victim compensation—are likely to become more effective than offender restitution.

Herbert Edelhertz notes that in its historic connotation, restitution was designed to benefit the offender rather than the victim.[5] Historically, restitution became the mechanism whereby the offender and his kin group made amends to the victim and his kin group and thus avoided a more severe sanction which the victim's kin group could legitimately impose. An interesting example of the same mechanism was recently reported in the Minnesota press.[6] An Ethiopian student murdered his roommate, another Ethiopian. The offender was found to be insane and committed to a program for the criminally insane after which the Immigration Service began deportation proceedings. The offender then requested a delay in his deportation until his family in Ethiopia could arrange a suitable settlement with the family of the victim (custom required that these negotiations could not begin until after a year of mourning had elapsed) so that he could safely return to Ethiopia without risk of being killed by the family of his victim.

A second purpose of restitution, which would be very consistent with its historic purpose, is to provide a less severe and more humane sanction for the offender. This purpose is implicit in diversionary programs and is more or less explicit in both the Minnesota and Georgia programs. The Minnesota Restitution Center is thought to be an alternative to imprisonment for property offenders and the Georgia Restitution Shelters are part of a package of programs that were funded in an effort to reduce the size of that state's prison population. Restitution as a mitigation of punishment requires consideration of the concepts of just deserts and parsimony.[7] Is restitution a just penalty for the crime and is it the least severe of appropriate penalties?

A third related, but conceptually distinct, purpose for restitution is rehabilitation of the offender. In the 1940s this purpose was advocated by I.E. Cohen,[8] and more recently by Albert Eglash,[9] Stephen Schafer,[10] O. Howbart Mower,[11] and Galaway and Hudson.[12] The rationale for speculating that restitution might be more rehabilitative than other correctional measures includes the notion that restitution is rationally related to the amount of damages done and thus would be perceived as more just by the offender. In addition, restitution is seen as specific and allowing for a clear sense of accomplishment as the offender completes concrete requirements; it requires the offender to be actively involved in the treatment program; it provides a socially appropriate and concrete way of expressing guilt and securing a sense of atonement; and through it the offender who makes restitution is likely to elicit a more positive response from persons around him than the offender sent to prison or receiving some other correctional sanction. In short, restitution is perceived as a sanction which enhances self-respect.

A fourth possible purpose for restitution is to benefit the criminal justice system by providing a fairly easily administered sanction permitting the reduction of demands on the system. Offenders can be rather easily processed while avoiding a public appearance of doing nothing or being "soft." While not articulated explicitly as a purpose, this rationale may be implicit in the use of restitution within informal diversion programs or as a probation condition.

A fifth purpose of restitution can be derived by speculating that the nature of the imposed criminal sanction reflects and has an impact on the overall society. Some sanctions may encourage brutality, divisiveness, and scapegoating. Others may lead to a sense of humaneness and further the integration of a society. One might argue that the restitution sanction may lead to a reduced need for vengeance and retribution in the administration of criminal law as offenders are perceived as responsible persons taking active steps to make amends for wrongdoing. If this is true, then perhaps the restitution sanction would have a positive impact on all of society.

These five possible purposes—redress for the victim, less severe sanction for the offender, rehabilitation of the offender, reduction of demands on the criminal justice system, and reduction of the need for vengeance in a society—are not mutually exclusive. Individual restitution programs, however, can reasonably be expected to specify the purpose or purposes for their existence.

Specification of Population

In addition to indicating the type and purpose of restitution, the program should specify the characteristics of the offender for whom the specified kind of restitution is thought to be an appropriate requirement in order to accomplish the program's purpose. The variables currently used by restitution projects to determine the suitability of offenders include the type of offense, age, extent of penetration into the criminal justice system, employability, and extent of damages resulting from the criminal offense. Regardless of the criteria, the characteristics of the offender for whom restitution is thought to be appropriate should be specified at the outset of the project.

But there is still another issue. Most existing restitution programs have used restitution as an add-on requirement. Restitution is combined with other correctional requirements—as a condition of probation, as a part of the program of a community corrections center, and so on. This subjects the offender to the usual requirements of these other correctional processes including, for example, mandatory counseling in the Minnesota Restitution Center. As the use of restitution expands, defining the appropriate relationship of restitution and other sanctions available to the criminal justice system will become an important policy issue. When is restitution a sufficient penalty? When and how should it be combined with other penalties? When should it not be imposed? An immediate evaluation problem for assessing the impacts of restitution is to identify a group of offenders for whom restitution is acceptable as the sole penalty. This will then permit study of the impact of restitution with less concern about possible contamination by other correctional requirements.

A crucial question then becomes: Can the process of requiring a specified group of offenders to make a specified type of restitution for a specified purpose under circumstances where restitution is the only correctional sanction required be undertaken in a setting which permits a reasonably controlled experiment? Minimally, can a portion of the specified population be assigned randomly to the restitution requirement with others' receiving the conventional criminal justice services in order to compare outcomes for the two groups? Before encouraging widespread adoption of restitution programming, a number of controlled experiments should be undertaken to test its impact. To this end, priority should be given to funding programs that can answer the following questions affirmatively:

1. Is the type of restitution requirement to be imposed clearly and stated explicitly?
2. Is the purpose or desired outcome of restitution clear?
3. Is the group of offenders for whom this type of restitution is thought to lead to the desired outcome clearly specified?
4. Is restitution the sole criminal justice sanction to be required of these offenders?

5. Is there a project evaluation design that will permit reasonably confident conclusions concerning the relation of restitution to the accomplishment of the purposes?

Descriptive Studies

In addition to the dissemination of information regarding current experience with restitution and moving toward controlled experimentation with the use of restitution, present programs suggest a number of questions for which exploratory and perhaps even qualitative research strategies are, at present, the most appropriate. Developers of restitution programs can contribute to the refinement and resolution of these issues by planning and implementing record-keeping systems that will enable administrators to share descriptive accounts of how their programs deal with several major questions. The questions can be grouped into three general areas: victim involvement, public acceptance, and impact on the criminal justice system.

Victim Involvement

What role, if any, should victims of crime play in a restitution program? If restitution is utilized as a less severe sanction, such as an alternative to imprisonment, what consideration should be given to the victim's wishes? This question has received almost no attention. Any program that attempts to actively involve the victim in the restitution process will be confronted with victims who, for a variety of reasons, decline participation. This raises the issue of whether the victim's failure to participate should serve as a veto over the offender's opportunity to utilize restitution instead of more severe sanctions. The Minnesota Restitution Center has resolved this issue by permitting the substitution of community service or payment of restitution to a community organization for the direct involvement of the victim. The Adult Diversion Project of Tucson, Arizona, however, permits either the victim or the arresting officer to veto the defendant's entry into a pretrial diversionary program utilizing restitution.

Existing programs range from those such as the Minnesota Restitution Center, The Iowa Restitution in Probation Experiment, and the Adult Diversion Project that attempt actively to involve the victim and the offender in direct communications both to develop a restitution plan and to continue contacts as the plan is implemented, to programs such as the Georgia Restitution Shelters in which court-ordered restitution is made through the intermediary of the shelter's business managers in order to avoid victim-offender contacts. The Iowa program represents an effort to deliberately introduce victim-offender involvement into a system in which restitution was already present but was being handled through court officials without victim-offender communication. To date the Minnesota experience indicates considerable success at securing the assistance of victims in negotiating the restitution contracts; less success, however, has been achieved in maintaining offender-victim communication once the contracts are completed and the offenders are actually implementing the agreement.[13]

The impact of victim-offender communication on both the victim and offender is at present unknown. This is an area that requires considerable further exploration. Can victims and offenders engage in meaningful contacts and communication that are beneficial to both? What does such communication do to the offenders perception of victims and the victims perception of offenders? Would such communication reduce the need for scapegoating and cries for retribution? These questions require experience and study that should develop as efforts continue to actively involve offenders and victims with each other.

The question of victim involvement raises two further issues—differentiating types of victims and consideration of victim culpability. Victims range from individuals to large organizations. Should the type of victim be a consideration in determining restitution obligations? How is "victim" to be operationalized in the case of large organizations? Does the type of victim influence the impact that restitution may be presumed to have on the offender or the willingness of the victim to be involved in a restitution program?

A growing body of evidence suggests that in some situations, victims may be partially responsible for their own victimization.[14] What part, if any, should the issue of victim culpability play in imposing restitution requirements? If a victim is partially responsible for victimization, does this influence the restitution obligation for the offender? How do victims' and offenders' estimates of loss vary? What is the possibility of victims' inflating the extent of their losses? Do offenders perceive victims as trying to "rip them off," and if so, how does this impact on the usefulness of restitution in achieving its stated purpose?

Public Acceptance

Another series of questions can be asked concerning the public acceptance of the restitution sanction. To what extent does the public perceive restitution as an appropriate sanction? Under what circumstances would the public accept restitution as a sole sanction, and under what circumstances should it be attached to other requirements? Do victims, as a subset of the public, perceive restitution as fair? To what extent are victims satisfied with restitution as the sole penalty? How do the public and victims perceive restitution vis-à-vis other criminal justice sanctions?

Impact on Correctional Programs

A final series of questions relate to the impact of restitution programming on other correctional programs. How does restitution programming influence the job of probation officers? To what extent is restitution compatible or incompatible with treatment approaches used in correctional services? Does a restitution requirement inhibit rehabilitation of offenders by detracting from ability to support self, family, or meet other financial obligations? Does it detract from counseling efforts directed toward inter or intrapersonal problems? Is restitution simply a bill-collecting procedure requiring little skill on the part of the correctional worker? When restitution is not the sole penalty, can it be integrated with other correctional services and sanctions for the offender? In the 1940s Irving Cohen suggested that restitution requirements provided a positive focus for the work of probation officers.[15] More recently Kathleen Smith has proposed that financial restitution (both directly to the victim and also to the society in the form of a court-ordered discretionary fine) become the basis for determining the length of time that an offender would be incarcerated.[16]

What is the cost of administering various types of restitution programs? What skills and tasks are necessary in implementing a restitution program, and how do these compare with the usual skills of correctional workers? Do some types of restitution reduce the need for other correctional services? Are there occasions when restitution may be an unjust sanction for the offender such as when an offense created damages so extensive that even the lifetime earning capacity of the offender might not be sufficient to make reparation? Also if some offenses and offenders are perceived as responding to an oppressive society, then an argument can be advanced that imposing a restitution requirement is just a continuation of the pattern of oppression (this argument, however, can also be advanced for any sanction that might be imposed under these circumstances).

These are some of the troublesome questions for which, at present, there are certainly no clear answers. Administrators of restitution programs can contribute to the development of a knowledge base in these areas by systematically recording and describing their experience in dealing with these issues. Simple surveys can be conducted to secure preliminary answers that can be tested out with experience. An immediate need is for the publication of good descriptive accounts of ways in which the questions are actually being resolved in practice and a description of the results that presumably flow from a particular resolution. From these accounts, more general principles can be developed to guide the further development of restitution programs.

Summary

This paper has identified three major research information needs necessary to the rational development of restitution in corrections: (1) assimilation and dissemination of the experiences in current restitution projects; (2) development of controlled experiments to begin testing the application of various types of restitution (this requires the development of operational definitions of restitution, a specific purpose of restitution, explicit definition of a population, preferably the utilization of restitution as the only sanction, and hopefully, a design in which random selection is acceptable; and (3) recording and publishing descriptive accounts of how questions in the areas of victim involvement, public acceptance, and impact on the correctional services are being answered as restitution is introduced in correctional programs. These descriptions should flow from operating programs and should describe both the actual practices of the program as well as the results observed from various practices. Restitution will continue to be formally and systematically utilized in corrections. With formal and systematic study of its use along with dissemination of materials, new programs will be spared the necessity of reinventing the wheel.

Notes

1. Janet Kole, "Arbitration as an Alternative to the Criminal Warrant," *Judicature* 56 (February 1973): 295-297; Carl Eklund, "The Problem of Overcriminalizing Human Conflict: A Civil Alternative Paper presented to the American Society of Criminology, November 1974, Chicago, Ill.

2. John W. Palmer, "Pre-arrest Diversion: Victim Confrontation," *Federal Probation* 38 (September 1974): 12-18.

3. Correspondence from Wilbert Long, Chief Juvenile Officer, Juvenile Court, St. Louis, Missouri, October 1975; and interview with Camden H. Raue, Offender-Victim Coordinator, Victims' Assistance Program, Pennington County Juvenile Court, Rapid City, South Dakota, August 1975.

4. Howard Standish Bergman, "Community Service in England: An Alternative to Custodial Sentence," *Federal Probation* 39 (March 1975): 43-46; John K. Harding, "Community Service—A Beginning," *Probation* (England) 19 (March 1973): 13-17; K. Pease et al., *Community Service Orders—A Home Office Research Report* (London: Her Majesty's Stationery Office, 1975).

5. Herbert Edelhertz et al., *Restitutive Justice: A General Survey and Analysis* Seattle: Battelle Human Affairs Research Centers, 1975), pp. 1-20.

6. Minneapolis *Tribune*, November 15, 1974, p. 1.

7. For a discussion of the concepts of deserts and parsimony, see Norval Morris, *The Future of Imprisonment* (Chicago: University of Chicago Press, 1974), pp. 53-84.

8. Irving E. Cohen, "The Integration of Restitution in the Probation Services," *Journal of Criminal Law, Criminology, and Police Science* 34 (1944): 315-321.

9. Albert Eglash, "Creative Restitution: A Broader Meaning for an Old Term," *Journal of Criminal Law, Criminology, and Police Science* 48 (1958): 619-622; "Creative Restitution: Some suggestions for Prison Rehabilitation Programs," *American Journal of Corrections* (November-December 1958): 20-22; Paul Keve and Albert Eglash, "Payments on a Debt to Society," *NPPA News* 36 (September 1957): 1-2.

10. Stephen Schafer, *Compensation and Restitution to Victims of Crime* (Montclair: Patterson Smith, 1970).

11. O. Hobert Mower, "Loss and Recovery of Community," in *Innovations to Group Psychotherapy*, ed. George M. Gazda (Springfield, Mass.: Thomas Press, 1968), pp. 130-148.

12. Joe Hudson and Burt Galaway, eds., *Considering the Victim: Readings in Restitution and Victim Compensation* (Springfield, Mass.: Thomas Press, 1975), pp. 59-70, 255-264.

13. Ibid., pp. 351-360.

14. Lynn A. Curtis, "Victim Precipitation and Violent Crime," *Social Problems* 21 (1974): 594-605.

15. Cohen, "The Integration of Restitution."

16. Kathleen Smith, *A Cure for Crime: The Case for the Self-Determinate Prison Sentence* (London: Gerald Duckworth and Co., Ltd., 1965).

7

Beyond Restitution—Creative Restitution

Albert Eglash

The Three Faces of Justice: Restitution Contrasted with its Alternatives

For thousands of years retributive justice and its technique of punishment for crime; for decades, distributive justice and its technique of therapeutic treatment for crime—these are the alternatives to restorative justice and its technique of restitution.

Often in bitter opposition to each other, these two alternatives are in many respects very similar to each other, but are in sharp contrast with a restitutional approach.

1. While both punishment and treatment concern primarily offenders' behavior, restorative justice focuses primarily on the destructive or harmful consequences of that behavior, its effect on the victims of the criminal act.

2. Similarly, while both punishment and treatment overlook the victims, except as witnesses, restorative justice makes victims and their needs an important consideration and gives them an important role to play both in achieving justice and in developing a rehabilitative or correctional program.

3. Both punishment and treatment place offenders in a passive role of receiving corrective action. An analogy is traditional medicine, where patients passively receive either surgery or some form of medication. By contrast, in restorative justice the basic requirement is an active, constructive effort on the part of the offenders themselves. We might use the analogy of biofeedback therapy as a treatment of medical disorders in which the patients heal themselves.

4. Both punishment and treatment remove offenders from the situation in which the offense occurred. *Creative restitution* keeps the offender in the situation but reverses his behavior from one of taking or harming to one of giving or helping.

5. The logic or rationale of our two traditional approaches require that, when successfully applied, misbehavior will stop, either because of deterrence, avoidance of punishment, or resolution of the underlying emotional conflict motivating the behavior. *Creative restitution*, as a form of guidance, recognizes that guidance does not prevent errors; it only destroys fixated patterns so that learning can begin to occur. In Alcoholics Anonymous, for example, a "slip" is not an indication of failure, but a painful opportunity to learn.

6. Both punishment and treatment define *past responsibility* in terms of the circumstances or causes of the criminal act; and when there is a question of possible insanity, are committed to a specific position regarding "free will" versus "psychological determinism." Similarly, both approaches define *present responsibility* in terms of vulnerability to social discipline, either punishment or treatment; and both insist that present responsibility is related to the past.

For example, jurists and theologians, accepting free will but rejecting psychological determinism, are likely to agree that we are responsible for our behavior, and as a consequence, we should be punished, in prison or in Purgatory for our willful disobedience of human or Divine law.

Similarly, behavioral and clinical scientists, accepting psychological determinism as part of the social sciences but rejecting free will as illusory are likely to agree that our developmental history and our metabolic and neurological condition, our cognitive-affective state at the time of the offense, were determinants of that offense and that since our behavior was determined by forces not under our own control, we are not responsible and should not be punished, but helped. Therapeutic treatment is seen both as just and as scientifically logical.

A restorative approach of *creative restitution* accepts *both* free will and psychological determinism. It redefines past responsibility in terms of damage or harm done, and can therefore accept psychological determinism for our past behavior without destroying the concept of our being responsible for what we have done. Similarly, it redefines present responsibility in terms of our ability or capacity for constructive, remedial action and can therefore accept free will for our present, ongoing behavior and for our future contemplated behavior, without destroying scientific explanations of past behavior. Only in restorative justice are determinations of past and present responsibility independent.

For instance, in AA, alcoholics insist "I'm not responsible for my past behavior, much of its most destructive moments occurring in a blackout when I was certainly far from sane. Still, I accept present responsibility to make amends to those I inadvertently hurt, and to help other victims of alcoholism."

If offenders are willing to make amends to their victims, then the classical question, "Was the defendant sane at the time of the crime?" becomes less crucial.

Four Types of Restitution

Once we make a decision that our main thrust will be neither toward retributive justice and punishment, nor toward distributive justice and therapeutic treatment of offenders but instead toward restorative justice and restitution, we may not have solved our problem of achieving both criminal justice and correctional rehabilitation; but, at least, we are now in a position to define our problem clearly: we can now begin to ask productive questions.

Perhaps the key question we ask becomes: "Do we want to compel the offender to make amends or do we want to leave it up to him to decide? Shall restitution be permissive or shall it be mandatory? Is the criminal free to choose or is he required?"

If we have only these two alternatives, then the alternative of freedom rather than of coercion is probably unacceptable to us. Given only these two alternatives, most of us will opt for making restitutional activity a requirement. But as soon as we make something a requirement, as soon as we coerce people, we find ourselves up against the stubborn perversity of the free human spirit, the rebel that lies within each of us.

Fortunately, we have four rather than two alternatives; for restitution is composed of two independent decisions, either one of which can be either free or coerced: first, a decision about making amends or not; second, what form the amends is to take.

1. In the *spontaneous restitution* of everyday life, both aspects are free: If deliberately or accidently I offend or harm someone, I am free to decide to make amends for what I have done, and I am equally free to decide how. In my opinion, spontaneous restitution has no important function in criminal justice or correctional rehabilitation.

2. In the *mandatory restitution* of civil court action, a court may require a defendant to make amends to his victim. Traditionally, for thousands of years this has taken the form of court-specified payments. Here both aspects are coerced: the defendant is required to make amends and told exactly how to do it. I doubt that financial reparations, in its usual form, has a great deal to contribute toward rehabilitation of an offender, although it provides a measure of justice for the victim of the crime.

3. It is not necessary that both aspects, both decisions, be either coerced or mandatory: One aspect can be free, the other required. For example, in *ritual restitution*, the decision about making amends is freely made; but, once made, the form is determined. This is the province of religion: I am free to select my religious affiliation for myself; but, once selected, I may find myself performing atonement rituals I did not choose for myself. These are designed more for reconciling man and God than for making amends to offended individuals.

Some clinicians, especially the psychoanalysts, have called attention to the ritual restitution of religion and the compulsive rituals, subtly restitutional in nature, of psychopathology: in the story, *I Never Promised You a Rose Garden*, a teenage girl has lost her hold on reality and, in compensation, creates an imaginary world. Analysts use the phrase, "loss and restitution."

4. Now we come to the last variety of restitution, and the one which I believe holds maximum promise for all of us concerned about justice to victim and offender alike, about rehabilitation of victim and offender alike—*guided restitution*, which I like to term, *creative restitution*.

In guided restitution, the offender is required to make amends for his offense, but is free to determine for himself what form this amends will take. At first glance, this may seem like a risky proceeding, for the offender may select some trivial gesture wholly disproportionate to his offense; and, if he does, then no useful purpose is served by the restitution.

However, if in addition to requiring restitution, we also define the restitutional act, then we leave the offender free only within the limitations of our definition. Let's look now at a definition of restitution that defines the act in terms of its characteristics.

Four Characteristics of Guided Restitution

Guided restitution is defined essentially as an offender's being required to make amends to the victim of his offense, while being free to select the form of the amends. Within this definition, we can distinguish some specific characteristics which the restitutional act has:

1. Restitution is an active, effortful role for the offender. This principle is well established in corrections, as when offenders do forestry or road-building work.
2. The active effort is also a constructive and helpful effort directed toward the victim of the offense.
3. The constructive or helpful aspect of the restitutional act is related to the nature of the damage or harm resulting from the offense. I know a juvenile court judge in Detroit who, when confronted with youths guilty of mischief against a railroad, had them visit the railroad operation daily and write about their observations. When other youths damaged a bus, he required them to help repair the damage and to weekly wash the bus.
4. The nature of the relationship between the restitutional act and the offense is reparative of damage done to person or property. For example, some youths caught vandalizing a park were required to plant and tend new trees.

Once we place these requirements on the amends, we protect the victim from a trivial act on the part of the offender. However, this does not protect the offender from vengeful demands on the part of the victim.

Two Characteristics of Creative Restitution

Were I inclined to be critical, as indeed I am, I would object that there is nothing essentially *creative* about the process of guided restitution. However, two further characteristics can be added which I believe justify describing the procedure as truly creative.

The Second Mile. The reparative effort does not stop at restoring a situation to its preoffense condition, but goes beyond: beyond what our own conscience requires of us, beyond what a court orders us to do, beyond what family or friends expect of us, beyond what a victim demands of us, beyond any source of external or internal coercion, beyond coercion into a creative act, where we seek to leave a situation better than it ever was.

I know a child who damaged a neighbor's mailbox. The girl's mother helped her to repair it, and together they restored it to its original condition, which wasn't very good. The next day, on her own initiative, she asked her mother for paint and brush, and she made the box more attractive than it had been prior to her act.

Another instance told to me by Paul Keve: After a long history as a chronic delinquent, Steve straightened out, and as a plumber, stayed out of trouble, married, and had a child. Then one day the sight of some copper tubing was too strong a temptation, and he stole it. Afterwards, sick and confused, he was glad to be caught.

Part of the probationary requirement was mandatory restitution for tubing stolen and used or sold. One day while waiting to make his regular payment, Steve overheard this: "Our club's constructing a playground for underprivileged kids, but we can't get the kind of tubing we need." On his own initiative Steve suggested the best source for the kind needed and then helped to construct the playground. In doing so, he helped to rebuild his own self-respect. His second mile took him back to the person he had hoped to be.

When we move into the realm of *creative restitution* and choose to walk a second mile, we resolve for ourselves the age-old philosophical dilemma of free will versus determinism. We begin to see that our destructive behavior was never freely chosen and was not our true self; that we ourselves have been victims of environmental pressures, of our own emotional pressures, of our misconceptions and destructive beliefs and attitudes; that our own thoughts, like a chattering monkey on our back whispering their stupid suggestions, betrayed us; that the behavior we thought we freely chose was in fact compelled; but that at the same time, we are indeed free to become as constructive as we wish.

As we gain this insight, seeing our offense as weakness, not as strength, we gain a sense of identification with others who are victims like ourselves; and we then extend the concept of "restitution to the victim" toward other offenders, themselves victims of those forces, external or internal, which alienate us from our own true self as well as from others.

Mutual Help Programs. I do not know if, literally speaking, there really exist demons who can possess us and who need to be exorcised. I am a hard-nosed skeptic. But at a figurative or emotional level, we are all at one time or another possessed by demonic forces. We all need help.

Part of *creative restitution* is the offender's activity on behalf of other offenders, a mutual-help relationship exemplified by the AA program: An alcoholic is likely to listen only to someone who has been through that same hell, and many delinquents prefer to listen to an excon rather than to a professionally trained worker. Moreover, an alcoholic's willingness to help other alcoholics stay sober may enable the helper to remain sober; an excon who tries to help delinquents not follow in his footsteps may be keeping himself out of trouble.

If this is so, then a largely untapped resource for helping offenders is other offenders. Bill Sands' Seventh Step Program is an example of this, and several years ago I helped get a similar program, Youth Anonymous, started in Detroit, under the leadership of an outstanding human being, Tip.

Tip had spent most of his life in correctional institutions—juvenile, state, federal, and military. He became dedicated to helping youth, and these youths listened to him when they scorned professional helpers.

Restitution in the Administration of Justice

The administration of criminal law begins when the police investigate a crime or a complaint and ends when an offender is discharged from probation, prison, or parole. At which points in this process can restitution appropriately fit?

In instances of minor complaints, restitutional activity may occur before any official criminal charge is brought; but, in more significant offenses, I think that restitution fits best as a probation requirement. Those who have already served time or who are still in prison often feel a sense of bitter resentment difficult to reconcile with restitution to victims.

However, I want to suggest one more point at which restitution may occur, namely, before any offense has been committed. I have encountered instances of preoffenders turning themselves in either to the police or to mental health agencies; and since the advent of community *hotlines*, we are in a good position to encourage preoffenders to seek help before committing any crime. I think that we can make amends even for a thought, an impulse; and some books on the psychological use of dreams suggest that, when a dream we have offended against anyone, we let them know about it.

The Differential Effect of Punishment and Restitution: A Controlled Experiment

I wrote two versions of a brief story describing a youngster stealing, caught, and disciplined by his parents, either by punishment or by guided restitution; then shuffled the two versions and distributed them randomly within a group of subjects.

Here is the story in its two versions, with the five questions and the percent of "yes" replies given to each question by the 203 subjects who happened to receive the punishment version and by the 209 subjects who happened to receive the restitution version.

A Story

Ten-year-old Jimmy steals a candy bar. The grocer catches him and tells his mother.

Punishment	Restitution
His mother makes him stay in the house that Saturday afternoon instead of going to a movie. He isn't allowed to have any candy for a week. His father spanks him.	His mother and father talk to Jimmy. They tell him to go back to the grocer and make up in some way for what he's done. Jimmy goes to the grover, apologizes, and offers to sweep out the store.

A few weeks later, Jimmy and another boy are in another store. His friend tells him how, without getting caught, Jimmy can take a bar of candy.

Questions	Percent of Yes Replies	
	Punishment	Guidance
1. Will Jimmy take the candy?	41%	27%

Discussion. This question attempts to measure the deterrence value of a disciplinary technique. Creative restitution seems to be regarded as more effective than punishment.

2. Does Jimmy feel that he got fair treatment from his parents?	52%	80%

Discussion. This question attempts to measure the deterrence value aspect of discipline. These results suggest that guidance is relatively effective in strengthening the relationship between child and parent.

3. The grocer needs a stockboy. Jimmy wants the job. Will he ask for it?	55%	76%

Discussion. Here we are attempting to measure self-acceptance in contrast with self-stigma. Apparently an offender feels humiliated, in part by the discipline to which he is subjected.

4. If he asks for the job, will he get it.	52%	73%

Discussion. Here we find that when creative restitution occurs, the victim apparently does not feel cheated at the thought of the offender "getting away with it," i.e., not being punished. Reconciliation is apparently more easily effected within a restitutional than within a retributional framework.

Questions	Percent of yes Replies	
	Punishment	Guidance
5. Jimmy's neighbors know what has happened. They are asked if Jimmy can, again this summer as he did last summer, stay with them for a week. Will they invite him?	67%	80%

Discussion. For an offender who is helped to make amends for his offense, social stigma is less.

Offenders' Attitudes

How do offenders themselves, those on probation or parole, those in prison or juvenile institutions, feel about the concept of restorative justice? I have talked with a large number, always in discussion groups, and have listened to their ideas and reactions. Here are some of the attitudes they express:

1. They have little respect for mandatory restitution and much prefer to have a say in the form the restitutional effort will take.
2. Even if they are free to select the form, they are reluctant to have restitution a requirement in addition to imprisonment: "I have already paid my debt to society."
3. Many see it as a good idea. "Yeah, it'd make me feel better." "Be hard to say, 'I'm sorry,' but I'm willing to give it a try."
4. Some see no need for it: "I didn't really hurt anyone, and the people I hurt, I'm not sorry about it."
5. Some are scared. "Naw, he might work me over. I don't know what I'm getting into."
6. Probationers are willing to accept it as part of the terms of probation, provided that a trusted mediator first approaches the victim and makes sure that the offender's gesture will be acceptable. An intermediary is needed.
7. Juvenile offenders especially seem to find the idea strange, as if no one—peers, parents, teachers, clergy—has ever told them: "If you wrong others, find a way to make it up to them." They, more than adults, want someone like Tip or a probation officer to pave the way.

The Victim

At the core of the restitutional concept lies the damage or harm done to victims of crime. In reading autobiographies of criminal offenders, I am impressed with their callousness toward their victims. Even when they determine, with apparent success, to pursue a different way of life, they never make amends to those they hurt.

The victim is generally overlooked. In a classroom experiment, I ask students how they would handle an incident of verbal or physical aggression, either name calling or actual violence. Invariably, they concern themselves solely with the aggressor, seldom with the victim.

I now want to admit that I too am offender oriented. From the start, I've been thinking and writing about ways to help offenders, about justice and rehabilitation for offenders. I work with and interview offenders. I seldom think about the victim, how to help him with his financial, medical, emotional, and social problems. I have never visited any victims, never interviewed any, never wondered what questions I would want to ask, never thought to include any victim interviews—"How do you feel about *creative restitution*?"—in this paper.

For me, restorative justice and restitution, like its two alternatives, punishment and treatment, is concerned primarily with offenders. Any benefit to victims is a bonus, gravy, but not the meat and potatoes of the process.

8

Community-service Restitution by Offenders

John Harding

The idea of community service by offenders is a comparatively recent development in the noncustodial treatment of offenders. Its legal origin lay in the report prepared by the Wootton Committee in 1970 on Non-Custodial and Semi-Custodial Treatment of Offenders. Community service was one of several recommendations put forward by the committee in an attempt to offer the government of the day some constructive alternative to prison and custody. The committee were made aware of the rising prison population in Britain, which by 1970 had reached 41,000. Penal reform groups and probation departments were pressing for community-based programs that offered some alternative to the courts for an adult facing a custodial sentence. On the strength of the committee's recommendation and the interest generated by the public at the time, the home office set up a working party to examine in some detail the feasibility of community service by offenders as an alternative to a shorter custodial sentence for men and women over the age of 17.

The Legal Framework of the Program

The community-service recommendations of the Wootton Committee, with some amendments, were finally incorporated in Section 15-19 of the Criminal Justice Act of 1972. This Act was later superseded by the 1973 Powers of Criminal Courts Act.

Following the report of the home office working party, the home secretary announced in the Summer of 1972 that community-service projects would be set up on a pilot-study basis in six probation areas—Nottinghamshire, Inner London, Kent, South West Lancashire, Durham, and Shropshire. The projects were designed to test out the feasibility of the courts making community-service orders. The six areas were given the authority to introduce community service to take effect on January 1, 1973. Each of the six areas was properly monitored from the start by the home office research team in Manchester, who were asked to evaluate the work of the community-service sections over a two-year period.

The main provisions in the 1973 Powers of the Criminal Court Act are as follows:

1. A person aged 17 years or over, convicted of an imprisonable offense, may be ordered to undertake unpaid work for any total number of hours

between 40 and 240, within a period of one year. Concurrent as well as additional orders are possible in respect of a number of different offenses, but the aggregate must not exceed 240 hours.

2. Orders may be made only with the offender's consent and where arrangements for orders in his area of residence have been approved by the Secretary of State and approval notified to that court. Courts must consider a probation officer's report about the offender, his circumstances, and the availability of suitable tasks, and if the court thinks necessary, his suitability to undertake such work.

3. An order must specify the Petty Sessions area in which the offender resides, and only a court acting for that area may deal with the subsequent amendments to the order, for example, breach or revocation proceedings, or when the change of the offender's circumstances compels transfer of the order.

4. Orders may be imposed by the magistrates courts or crown courts.

5. The requirements of the order and the legal provisions for breach or revocation procedures, etc., must be explained to the defendant by the court before the order is made. Copies of the order must be passed to the probation officer who must serve a copy on the offender. The requirements are that the offender must report to the relevant officer as instructed, and notify him of any change of address; and that he shall perform for the number of hours specified such work at such times as he may be instructed by the relevant officer.

6. Instructions for work should, as far as practicable, avoid interference with the offender's normal work, education or religious activities.

7. Breach of a requirement of an order, if proved, may attract a fine not exceeding £50, without prejudice to the continuation of the order.

8. Revocation of an order, whether for breach of requirements or under other circumstances, may be dealt with by way of any penalty that could have been imposed for the original offense. Where breach of requirement is not involved, courts may simply revoke the order without further penalty.

9. Schedule III of the Act outlines the provisions for the appointment of a community-service subcommittee of a probation and aftercare committee, and the powers of the subcommittee. The community-service subcommittee acts as a policy controller for the organization of community service in a probation area. The committee is made up of lay magistrates and certain ex officio members such as a trade-union official, chairman of a volunteer bureau, a judge, a journalist, plus the senior probation personnel responsible for the administration of the scheme.

The Organization of the Service

Each of the six experimental community-service areas has by circumstances and emphasis brought something different to the scheme. Inner London operates on a scale nearly twice as large as that of any other area. Kent has a particular philosophy of operation involving a detailed allocation procedure before place-ment with a voluntary agency. Nottinghamshire emphasizes integration of community service with the numerous voluntary organizations in the area. Durham shares Nottinghamshire's emphasis and the community-service office had to be active in stimulating voluntary effort. Durham and Shropshire are largely rural areas, with problems of travel. The scheme in South West Lancashire operates in an area with pockets of very high unemployment and so uses weekday work more than do other areas.

Thus, because areas have different local pressures and different policies to accommodate these pressures, they have all developed separate perspectives on the scheme since the beginning of the experimental period. However, the scheme has proved viable in that work is being done and orders are being completed in all the areas.

All six areas have expanded into new court areas since the beginning of the scheme. Three of them—Durham, Nottingham, and Kent—now have two admin-istrative centers. Each scheme involves allocating offenders to work that may be provided by voluntary agencies, statutory authorities, agencies stimulated into existence by the community-service office, or by the probation and aftercare service itself. Offenders on community service are supervised either by members of the work-providing agency or by full-time or sessionally paid probation staff. Supervision may be continuous, intermittent, or nominal, depending on the nature of the task and the behavior of the offender.

The senior probation officer is in day-to-day charge of the scheme. He is accountable to the chief probation officer and the community-service commit-tee. The senior probation officer, or community-service organizer as he is usually known, is involved in locating tasks, matching and allocating offenders to the tasks, liaising with work-providing agencies, sentencers and probation officers, following-up difficult offenders and initiating breach proceedings in the courts. He is also responsible for a team of probation officers who are involved in similar work. As these schemes have expanded, more staff have been recruited. It is currently estimated that a staff member is responsible for between 40 and 50 offenders on community service. Areas also appointed full-time ancillary staff whose tasks included the organization of equipment and transport, supervision of small work groups, follow-up and liaison with community groups, and follow-up with offenders for breach requirements. In Nottinghamshire, an additional staff resource was obtained from the local Council of Voluntary Service, where the services of the volunteer bureau organizer were used to place some offenders. The bureau maintained good contacts with a number of local groups and thus afforded community-service section with additional outlets.

In all areas local probation officers are advised to contact the community-service office before recommending community service to the court. Careful matching of an offender to an available task is made before the first work allocation. The offender's experience in that first work task confirms his suitability or unsuitability for that type of work; if he is unsuitable, other work placements are tried. As a general rule, an offender remains in one allocation throughout his order, if the work continues to be available and he responds well.

The community-service office's contact with offenders on community service is maintained through supervisors; the community-service organizers themselves do not often see the offender after the induction interview and initial matching, unless, for example, the offender requires help of a personal nature or breach proceedings are being contemplated. In Nottinghamshire the community-service organizer interviews each offender in the middle and end of his order to ascertain his response and attitude to the scheme.

Research reveals that over 60 percent of offenders on community service are supervised by nonprofessional staff, voluntary group or community organization. The remainder are supervised by sessional supervisors employed by the probation service. The sessional supervisors take responsibility for small working parties of offenders, usually at the weekend or in the evening. Tasks include painting and decorating houses and flats for the elderly and physically handicapped, making toys and equipment in a workshop base for the handicapped and disabled, and special project work on adventure playgrounds or community centers. Sessional supervisors are drawn from many quarters; some are tradesmen or craftsmen, some are well-motivated students, and, significantly, some are exoffenders who have graduated through the community-service scheme to the point where they are assessed as suitable for the leadership role. Other supervisors within the voluntary sector are, in the main, ordinary men and women from the community who give their time to a particular voluntary organization.

The task of the supervisor, whether voluntary or sessional, is crucial in that he undertakes the direct work with the client and carries out the intentions of the court in relation to the offender. Beyond this, however, the realization of the spirit of community-service orders lies in the hands of the supervisor, who conveys to the offender not only the expectations of the community but also the value of the task he is undertaking and the appreciation of the community for his efforts. The use of nonprofessional staff in community-service schemes has been recommended during the experimental period (1) for reasons of economy of resources, (2) because it creates a role for those committed to the idea of work with offenders but not trained for it, and (3) because the nonprofessional is capable of a special contribution in being seen by the offender as more sincere and more representative of the attitude of the community as a whole. None of these virtues can be denied, but it should be emphasized that the successful use of nonprofessional staff depends very much on the clear identification of the distinction between professional and nonprofessional tasks, and availability of skilled support for such workers. While the demands on the community-service team for direct support of clients may be more limited, every client has a supervisor who will require some degree of support through the order.

Regular contact is maintained with nonprofessional supervisors on a weekly basis either by written or spoken communication. Each week a supervisor returns a worksheet that gives details of a person's attendance at and performance on the task. On average, an offender performs approximately eight hours service a week whether in the evening or on the weekend. Regular visits are made to the organizations to obtain progress reports on an offender's placement. A further quarterly meeting of sessional supervisors and other nonprofessionals is held at the office headquarters. Such meetings may be divided into specialist groups. For example, one might hold a meeting of those supervisors working in youth groups, organizations for the handicapped, or those supervisors responsible for small work parties. Nonprofessional staff are not expected to attend court and give evidence on someone who has breached a requirement. In the event of an unsatisfactory placement, an offender is returned to a work party supervised by one of the probation ancillary staff. If he further offends in this group, then evidence is given to the court by the probation staff member.

The Rationale and Purpose of the Program

In the second reading debate in the House of Commons on the 1972 Criminal Justice Bill, the then home secretary said,

I was attracted from the start by the idea that people who have committed minor offenses would be better occupied doing a service to their fellow citizens than sitting alongside others in a crowded gaol. This will, of course, have to be a voluntary choice of the individual concerned for a number of reasons; afterall, if it is not done voluntarily, the work will not be good. The alternative will be to go to gaol.

Later in committee, an Under-Secretary of State said,

I know that it is the personal wish of the Home Secretary that not only should the scheme work, but that it should be a type or order which the courts may come to use freely and one which they will turn to as a normal alternative to a short custodial sentence as a means of making people pay for their offenses rather than merely spend a short time, of a probably not very reformative nature, in an overcrowded local prison.

Thus the principal intention of the 1972 Criminal Justice Act was to reduce the number of persons committed to custodial institutions.

Among other assumptions made at the outset, one can list the following:

1. In cost terms, community service is a cheaper alternative to prison or borstal or detention center. In Great Britain the average cost of keeping a man in prison is currently £45 per week. An average length order of 120 hours takes approximately 6½ months to complete and costs £158.

2. Community service allows an offender to live in the community with his wife and family, supporting them by his normal work.
3. It avoids some of the more negative effects of prison: overdependence, loss of decision making, loss of responsibility, loss of status.
4. It gives an offender an opportunity to contribute in some form in the community, and thereby gain status and approval for his actions.

The last assumption represents the kernel of the community-service philosophy. The notion of using the offender as a community resource was not in itself novel since scattered experiments have been taking place in Britain and the United States in the sixties and early seventies. In the United States, the Kennedy/Johnson era had seen the launching of the ambitious community-development programs in large urban areas like New York, where the ghetto resident faced environmental deprivation on a multiple scale. Community workers within these projects began hiring local residents from disadvantaged areas or organizers and social work aides, often with great effect. The New Careers Movement spread in the United States to include employment schemes for exoffenders, ghetto residents, and the poor. Similar approaches were adopted in Britain at the start of the seventies. Five borstals working in conjunction with the community-service volunteer organization in London sent a number of trainees during their sentence to work in homes for old people or centers for the handicapped. The community-service-by-offenders scheme shared a similar philosophy to those other projects in attempting to make people dispense a service rather than become recipients of help.

Other treatment possibilities may be claimed for community service, although it may not be the only possible method in any one case. It may combat social isolation on almost any level, including the isolated and often institutionalized offender, whose only community is behind prison walls. It may give him a sense of belonging to the world outside prison. It may help the offender who lives in a community to which he feels he does not belong, either because he offends or because he lacks achievement or a particular skill or identity that is traditional in his family. He can be enabled to demonstrate similar skills, or establish entirely new ones. He may even have a family that is isolated, but who can become more active in the community with the offender such as when wives accompany their husbands to help at voluntary organizations. Offenders, too, learn to work in a group wherever they are placed for community service. Experience shows that the practical work group composed of four to six offenders and a supervisor appears invariably to develop positive social value. Within this setting, many offenders tested their own behavior and attitudes against the reactions of their fellow workers and have begun to achieve a more generally acceptable level of functioning. These groups can be appropriately critical or supportive, often helping to resolve members' personal problems without recourse to statutory sources. Within the groups themselves, therefore, there may develop a microcosmic concept of community, and the elements of concern for others.

By contrast, community-service tasks that involve direct help to the severely disadvantaged such as the mentally and physically handicapped, children at risk, the elderly and sick, may be seen as a very appropriate treatment method for an admittedly small but distinct group of offenders. The reparative element in community service can help an offender to shed a burden of guilt—not only the obvious guilt deriving from some damage he may clearly have done to others by an offense, but the often inexplicable guilt derived from some forgotten action or omission. More commonly, perhaps, among those who undertake direct service to the disadvantaged, we can perceive the symptoms of growing maturity, the development of a capacity to have concern for others, the move away from the egocentricity of the child. This aspect is particularly important in view of the large proportion of our intake who are in their late adolescent years.

Certain rather practical benefits also emerge from community service. It gives opportunities for offenders to identify skills and work interests that they themselves did not suspect or regard as useful. It may help to identify entirely new skills, when existing ones are no longer appropriate or in demand, or test an interest or aspiration before the offender commits himself to lengthy training or employment. To a limited extent, it can be used to help the chronically unemployed to reestablish a work habit. Finally, it is possible via community service to offer a more constructive use of leisure to those who, because of mental or physical handicaps or social factors, are unable to work, and at the same time counteract isolation.

Central Issues Involved in the Implementation of the Program

In setting up a community-service program, the organizer faces three main tasks. They include:

1. The community acceptance of the program and the identification of the tasks;
2. The cooperation of the courts, particularly magistrates, judges, and clerks to the justices;
3. Cooperation and involvement of colleague probation officers and other social workers in the community.

The organizer needs to maintain an essential balance between these separate but interconnected tasks. If cooperation breaks down on any one of these three essential tasks, the whole scheme is in jeopardy. From the outset, therefore, the organizer proceeds with the assumption that he will work with three separate interest groups at different levels using skills that are not unfamiliar to the community worker.

Community Acceptance

The author was appointed as Community Service Organiser in Nottinghamshire three months prior to the opening of the scheme on January 1, 1973. The contacts with the community organizations usually involved a meeting with the representative of the organization concerned, at which community service was explained in some detail. From such meetings it was determined whether the agency would be able to provide suitable work for offenders, and also what was the attitude of the agency toward community service and the use of offenders generally. In many cases, more than one meeting was needed before a decision was reached, because the proposal had to be put to a committee or because more information was required. Some agency representatives wanted time to think about the implications of the scheme, or practical issues such as insurance had to be clarified. Some agencies simply did not have suitable work for offenders. During the period October 1972 to January 1974, 152 agencies were approached. Of these, 54 reacted favorably and were able to provide work and a further 75 were favorable but the provision of work was uncertain. Of the remainder, 5 were unfavorable but open to further negotiation, 1 was unfavorable and not open to any further negotiation, and 16 had no clear outcome. Thus the reception of the idea of community service ranged in nearly all cases from great enthusiasm to willingness to give the scheme a trial. A member of another organization, who had the most reservations about community service during a meeting, was the one who afterwards suggested further possible contacts for the scheme.

The interviews with the community service officers gave some indication of the attitude of voluntary agencies toward community service. The main reason for agencies being reluctant to participate appeared to be their feelings towards offenders working as volunteers; for example, one organization had had an unhappy experience in using Borstal boys. Alternatively, they may feel threatened by the thought of using offenders or that the good name of the agency would be contaminated by doing so. On the other hand, the agency may simply have wanted to wait until it had seen the scheme in operation before committing itself. In practice it was easier to establish links with voluntary organizations and local tenant groups than with local authority departments and local hospitals. The process of acceptance was slower in local authority committees, as they discussed the implications of the experiment in detail. Officials could easily accept the offender in a practical role but raised difficulties when asked to find tasks that involved relationship skills such as visiting the elderly in hospitals, or befriending a mongol child. The barrier was broken by the education department youth workers who were willing to use offenders as assistant leaders in youth club settings. Subsequently, offenders have pioneered new developments with local authority departments. They can now be found working in children's homes, running day centers, assisting in preschool play groups, and organizing intermediate treatment activities alongside probation officers and social workers.

On a public relations note, the organizer lost no opportunity to make contact with civic leaders, trade-union officials, and the media. Numerous talks were given to local organizations, debating societies, Rotary groups, etc. Although many of these groups expressed divergent opinions about the usefulness of community service, the idea attracted widespread support which was maintained throughout the two-year experimental period.

Relationship with the Courts

One of the first major issues confronting magistrates and judges was to ascertain the place of community service in the range of sentencing alternatives for imprisonable offenses. As has been made clear, when the Criminal Justice Bill was being debated in the Houses of Parliament, ministers saw community service primarily as a method of dealing with persons who might have been sent to prison for shorter periods of imprisonment. In three of the six experimental areas, the chief probation officer, or working groups set up by them, have tended to view community service primarily as, or only as, an alternative to custody. In the other three areas, community service is regarded as having a wider use, and in one of these the position is defended by the argument that if community service is primarily an alternative to custody, the probation officer writing the social inquiry report must expect that the court will consider making a custodial sentence before he would be in a position of recommending the alternative of community service. In Nottinghamshire, for example, magistrates and judges agreed to confine community-service orders to those who might have been given a custodial sentence. Some attempt was made thereafter to introduce an unofficial tariff system, whereby a person whom magistrates felt might have received a 12-month prison sentence would be given an order for 240 hours. In the same way, 120-hour order might be equivalent to a 6-month prison sentence. In practice the policy became a flexible instrument with a good deal of variation, often depending on the attitudes and approach of the respective magistrates. As the scheme developed, it was suggested that the court should assess hours in terms of (1) the gravity of the offense and previous record of convictions, and such other matters as would normally be weighed in passing sentence; (2) the capacity of the offender to take some regular responsibility for his attendance over an extended period; and (3) the extent of his work and domestic responsibilities and other pressures he may be facing.

Sentencers, for example, have been discouraged by probation staff from making long orders—upwards of 200 hours—on young offenders whose ability to work through such an order was found to be limited. The same tendency can be discerned in the recidivist with long institutional experience. Once these and other concerns about the possible effects of the length of an order had been identified, it became the practice to encourage probation officers to offer details to courts on the suitable length of an order in their reports. The response of courts to this practice has been encouragingly positive, and it has become clear that the imposition of maximum orders (which may present particular difficulty simply because they are the maximum) has been reduced considerably, and that those that are made without reference to the offender's capacity to undertake them are made now in the absence of specific advice from the reporting probation officer. It is felt that the willingness of courts to adopt the advice of the probation service in this instance can by extension be taken to demonstrate their general confidence in the content of social inquiry reports.

Possibly a larger issue among sentencers during the initial planning meetings was a dispute about the overall aims of community service. Some saw community service as a punishment whereby the offender could repay his debt to society. Others saw the measure in more personalized terms as a method of rehabilitation. Ironically, the notion of community service gained a certain unifying strength amongst magistrates through its appeal to conflicting philosophies about crime and punishment.

Other questions were directed to the type of task the offender might undertake. There were some objections to the task that brought offenders into direct personal contact with the young, handicapped, or elderly. Some voiced criticism that helping in a club for the handicapped was a soft option alongside the more practical task of digging a garden. The organizer was placed in a position of now having to defend his ground. Other magistrates took issue with their colleagues who shared this view. Work with the handicapped, they maintained, could make mental and emotional demands on an offender that were far from soft or easy in terms of commitment.

On the whole, magistrates lent their support to the community-service scheme, but support could have faded quickly if preparations were not made to supply magistrates with a flow of information about the progress of the scheme. Information sheets were sent to each magistrate at the outset. This gave details of the tasks and the organizations who had agreed to participate in the experiment. Individually, magistrates were at liberty to ask probation officers at the time of the court proceedings for a follow-up review of a person made the subject of a community-service order. Some magistrates enjoyed even closer contact with those on community service. A number of magistrates were associated with voluntary organizations as active participants. Some have worked alongside offenders and shared tasks at day centers, clubs for the handicapped, and youth clubs. None, to our knowledge, have revealed their other responsibility to the offender and thus have felt able to mix and share experiences as ordinary volunteers.

The Role of the Probation Service

There was some skepticism in the probation service, both locally and nationally, when the legislative details of community service were first announced. Officers questioned the assumption behind the measure. The essence of voluntary work in the community is of service freely given without any element of compulsion. Were not community-service orders, therefore, a contradiction in terms? How could one compel an offender to give up his leisure time to some form of service? Probation officers were quick to point out that although the offender had to give consent to the making of an order, in reality it was Hobson's choice since the alternative option was prison or another type of custodial sentence. In addition, anxieties were raised by the type of tasks that would be made available to the offender. Would it be a repetition of the Victorian chain gang?

All these questions suggested that the organizer should spend much of his time with local teams exploring and discussing the measure in some depth. Out of these meetings came requests for further information and clear guidelines about the running of the project. A community-service working party was set up two months before the start of the scheme on a cross-representational basis from all the area teams. This group, together with the community-service section staff arranged to meet monthly so that information could be shared and policy questions raised. Having looked at some of the anxieties present at the outset, the organizer's next task was to help probation officers to look at the selection of suitable offenders for the scheme. One relied on the probation officer's skill in assessment as an essential feature in starting a new sentencing venture. From this process, two problems were identified. The first is to avoid the creation of a limited understanding of the new method. Inevitably a new method must be preceded by a tested prediction about its scope and applicability, but its potential becomes stunted if all those involved are not kept in touch with the understanding that emerges from actual practice. In some ways, the possibilities presented by community service are so novel—particularly in the opportunity they offer to identify and mobilize the offender's positive quality in contrast to traditional attempts to minimize his defects and limitations—that there is a genuine risk that the full scope of the measure might not be explored. Consequently, it is seen as essential to develop effective methods of communicating to probation officers the relevance of their recommendations in order that they in turn may better advise the courts in future instances.

The second problem in establishing a new measure like community service relates to involvement in the rewards of the work undertaken. Probation officers commonly see people who fail to respond to the skills they exercise in supervision. In some respects, those who are responsible for community service are in the unenviable position of experiencing directly the value of their work. Beyond the important reward of seeing an offender complete a community-service order, the staff receive frequent evidence of the offender's positive achievement; it is sometimes difficult to choose between the pleasure created by the offender's sense of achievement or that created by the enthusiastic support of the group from whom he has taken work.

Both these problems of communication can be avoided only by the creation of close links between the specialist team undertaking community-service work and those responsible for providing an intake. The responsibility for maintaining such communication rests with the community-service team, but the effectiveness of the link depends entirely on the willing participation of the probation service as a whole. The pattern of communication includes the pretrial consultation, the regular provision of progress reports to the officer who recommended an order, and, in those instances where two forms of involvement with an offender exist, as close a liaison as possible between the two officers involved.

Aspects of Selection, Assessment, and Matching

At the outset, community service organizers were asked to detail those offenders, felt to be suitable or unsuitable to the scheme. The following guidelines were drawn up.

Not Suitable
a. The psychotic or highly disturbed
b. The heavily addicted—drugs or alcohol
c. Those who have committed a serious sexual offense
d. Those of very low intelligence
e. Those who are facing a crisis situation which would suggest probation as a more suitable alternative

Suitable
a. The isolated and withdrawn
b. Those lacking in social training who need an experience of consistency and continuity
c. Seriously disadvantaged people whose offenses might be related to lack of opportunity at various stages in their lives
d. Those whose crimes may be serious but whose background is fairly stable
e. Actors-out, chip-on-shoulder, low self-esteem, purposeless livers who are always on the receiving end and believe that the world owes them a living.

As the Nottinghamshire project developed, we became less bound by those early exclusions. We have been able to include in the scheme, quite successfully, two registered addicts, three severely handicapped offenders, and several people with drinking problems. Some voluntary organizations have shown remarkable resilience in coping with them to the extent that earlier reservations have been substantially modified.

Screening procedure is as follows. The probation officer, having examined the various points of suitability for community service, makes contact with the community-service organizer and discusses the case in hand. The latter is concerned to know something of the offender's response to the idea of community service. He also asks a series of practical questions that cover a person's work pattern, available leisure time, attitude of family and friends, and the nature of the offense. The community-service organizer finally offers some advice about recommendation and informs the officer that suitable tasks are available. The important feature of this process is then recorded in the probation officer's written report to the court. The responsibility for initiating community-service recommendations can be either through the initiative of a magistrate or judge at an early court hearing or by the direct recommendation of a probation officer through contact with a client whom he knows is going to court.

The assessment and matching of offenders to tasks is a crucially important aspect of the scheme. Offenders are seen within days of the making of the order at the community-service headquarters. The interviewer is already in possession of a social inquiry report, but this in itself is of limited value in terms of making an assessment. Somehow within the framework of the first interview, the organizer has to put across the requirements of the order and convey the spirit of community service. The offender has already given his consent to community service, but that agreement took place in a court room. It would be misleading to assume that an agreement of that kind was a reflection of a person's motivation toward community service. Motivation, therefore, does not automatically follow from a legal sentence. A setting has to be created in which the offender gradually becomes aware of the significance of community service both for others and himself. Often this process takes weeks, months to achieve. Sometimes the offender is scarcely motivated at all but will perform the hours to meet the requirements of the sentence. One has learned not to assume too much about a person's response on a first encounter. Changes take place in a person's response over a period of time so that the first and last assessment on that person could reflect different attitudes. (See Appendix 8A, Case Illustrations.)

In the first interview there is a deliberate focus on a person's activities and interests. One is concerned to know something of a person's coping ability. Attitude to work, leisure, family, and friends are of some significance in helping to draw up a picture of likely response to community service. Questions are asked about their ambitions. Many of those interviewed display a wide gap between their present reality and future aspirations for themselves. Others reveal a more personal response to questions about the future. One young man replied, "I just want to be someone." Another woman in her early thirties with five children in care said, "I'd like to feel I was of some use. I've lost my self-respect." The last two comments, so typical of many we have seen, indicate a need for recognition that could, in part, be met by the type of placement we arrange.

Some reference is also made to previous experience of helping others. We avoid the use of the word *volunteer* in this question as many would not identify simple examples of befriending with the role of volunteer. Almost all those interviewed have some experience of this kind to draw on. Often such details have never been raised in the context of their relationship with the previous supervising officer. Following these questions, attention is then drawn to the task list (see Appendix 8B). Offenders are asked to nominate those roles on the list that would most interest them. Responses vary. Some opt for a group of personalized tasks, others follow more practical orientation. A few would prefer to continue both practical and personal roles within the task. This is not difficult to arrange, as with some organizations the line between personal and practical is very thin. The offender's choice of task will be strongly taken into consideration along with several other factors such as age, nature of his offense, public risk, and degree of motivation. Final arrangements are made between the organizer and the placement organization. We try as far as possible to arrange placement to meet the assumed needs of each individual. For example, Andrew, disabled in his left leg as a result of polio, was placed with a sports club for the physically handicapped as a volunteer leader. Andrew had come to terms with his disability and was able to offer considerable help and encouragement to youngsters with similar problems. Such matching is not always easy due to a number of factors. Sometimes one is uncertain about a particular offender so he may be placed in a practical task with a work party to test out his response. On other occasions the appropriate task may not be available. Similarly, some organizations undergo changes in personnel so that the organizer is forced to hold off placing people until some stability has been reached.

Offenders are usually placed with organizations or practical work groups within a week to three weeks of their first assessment interview. During the interim the community-service organizer has been in touch with the supervisor responsible for an organization to gain his total agreement to a placement. There is no onus on the placement agency to accept an offender. They will often reserve judgment until the subject has been informally interviewed by their nominated supervisor. The organizer gives some details of the offender to the organization, including the offense, name, age, address, known abilities, and any other relevant information thought to be of some value to the organization. Organizations do not require personal dossiers and are usually content with bare, essential details so that they can form uncluttered opinions for themselves. Most of the organizations have accepted an offender as an ordinary volunteer not to be differentiated in any way from other members of the serving public. The detailed information about a person remains with only two or three key members of the group. This degree of acceptance and trust has been one of the chief factors in contributing to the success of the scheme. Naturally, if an offender wishes to tell his story, he is free to do so. Many do, possibly to test out initial overtures of acceptance within a group. Such sharing can create a more realistic dialogue between the offender and the group. But the decision must rest with the offender.

The Role of the Community

As has been illustrated in a previous section, community organizations and groups responded from the outset to the challenge of community service by offenders. Some general reflections on this relationship follow. Experience has shown that while offenders working as volunteers in outside organizations should not be singled out publicly as offenders, they do require a special degree of reassurance as to the value of their contribution. It is not always possible to convey to offenders adequately at the beginning of an order that organizations will value them for their work. Even before starting work, offenders often ask whether they would be allowed to continue on a voluntary basis after their orders were completed. Community-service staff have always accepted the importance of the responsibility to enable such a development as continuity, and it is interesting to note that in the first 18 months of the Nottinghamshire scheme, approximately 35 percent of offenders completing orders remained with the organization as a volunteer afterwards. It became apparent, however, that attempts at permanent involvement of offenders beyond the requirements of the order are not best undertaken via the obvious intervention of community-service staff themselves. Only the spontaneous appreciation of the organization and the beneficiaries for whom he is working will be seen as trusted and real.

The importance of this particular aspect, that is, the extent to which the offender feels valued for his work, can also be seen in relation to probation-organized tasks. Here, while it is not always possible to guarantee the opportunity to work alongside other volunteers, the essential opportunity for the offender to test the attitude of the community can be incorporated in several ways. Possibly the role of the sessional supervisor, as a representative of the community without specialized social work training has at times been under-estimated. Sessional supervisors have clearly demonstrated their understanding of this role. In particular, a number of former offenders have been employed as supervisors and the expectation that this would lead to the creation of work groups with antisocial values has not been borne out. In addition, the opportunity to experience the impact of their work on the beneficiary is usually available, although occasionally only via the representative of an organization concerned. It has sometimes been necessary to investigate poor response or work by a particular group, and this has almost invariably been found to be associated either with a direct expression of lack of appreciation by the beneficiary, or with the evidence that the extent of the beneficiary's need has been exaggerated. On the other hand, there have been a number of instances where a work group, on perceiving the real extent of a beneficiary's need, have without direction far exceeded their brief to help that person, occasionally refusing to be credited with hours for doing so.

The apprehension of the community about dealing directly with the offender is real and widespread, and it is to the credit of many work-providing organizations that they are so willing to experiment in spite of evident anxieties and misgivings, rather than in the absence of these. Obviously, their actual experience with offenders has not always been satisfactory, but the usual course for the removal of an offender from a particular task has been unreliability of attendance rather than unacceptable work or behavior. This in itself demonstrates the high level of commitment of organizations to offenders under their supervision and the extent to which they must have modified their demands on the offender's actual ability. As far as the offender is concerned, unreliability can usually be attributed to deficiencies in the matching process or the original assessment of the offender, although it should be emphasized that accurate predictions of the offender's ability and response are never possible, and every matching process is likely to be to some extent an act of faith on the part of the community-service team, the outside organization, and the offender himself. Unreliability may occur because the demands on the offender are too great or too little, or because of domestic health or employment factors, or traveling difficulties unconnected with the placement. It may, of course, also derive from an offender's refusal to stick to the requirements of the order.

Instances of unacceptable behavior by offenders at work locations are extremely rare, and it is usually possible to trace these to a history of mental instability or evidence of general unsuitability for community service. Instances of actual material loss sustained by a beneficiary through contact with offenders appears to be even more rare. Any apparent losses reported are thoroughly followed up, and it must be said that sometimes such losses turn out to be the result of hasty assumptions about an article temporarily mislaid. It is believed that during a period when about 500 offenders in Nottinghamshire had been the subject of orders, and several thousands of hours of work undertaken, only four instances of theft had occurred, one of which was property belonging to the probation service, two which were property belonging to sessional supervisors, and one which was a direct theft from a member of the public. The individuals sustaining such losses were compensated.

As confidence grew in the scheme, one was able to cope with the occasional negative comment in the press. A correspondent once wrote to a Nottingham evening newspaper that the thought of burglars doing social service work filled him with horror. He signed his letter "chop off their hands." A week later a councillor replied. He was chairman of the Nottingham City Education Committee. Thirty offenders were placed with youth organizations in the first 18 months. His reply: "All concerned with the scheme are convinced community service represents a significant break-through in terms of reducing the prison population as it offers an offender the opportunity to play a useful and worthwhile role in society." But the most rewarding acclaims for the project came from the local secretary of a community care group.

I have been asked by the passengers of the community bus to write to you on their behalf to thank you for Colin and the wonderful work he is doing. He is not only an artist at driving. He has that reassuring personality so essential when taking invalids who have not ventured out of their homes for some time. His skill and indefinable something has made these people ask to be included trip after trip. Many passengers expressed their affection for him in tangible ways by inviting him and his family to tea, etc.

That care group, for example, started off with one community-service offender, Colin. Twelve months later, this voluntary organization was using the services of ten offenders in the evenings and the weekends. They were mainly involved in providing bus trips and organizing a shopping service and a program of household repairs for the housebound elderly and disabled.

Thus experience in Nottinghamshire has necessitated the revision of a number of assumptions about the community attitude and response to offenders. There is no further need to canvass community organizations for tasks. The opposite is the case; the community-service staff are constantly having to turn away requests for help because of insufficient numbers of offenders on the scheme at any one time. The ability of organizations to balance offenders' needs with their own is a source of constant surprise to the community service staff. It has been found that sharing communication of the kind outlined makes special demands on the time and resources of all those involved, and requires a degree of mutual confidence and respect that can easily be underestimated. While organizations have accepted responsibility toward the offender, the community-service team have learned to identify their own, sometimes far-reaching, responsibilities to the community—to protect and support the efforts of other organizations without usurping their functions, to ensure continuity of service when this is essential to the existence of an organization, and to act as a focal point for exchange of information and the extension of cooperation between different groups.

Some Additional Data and Evaluation Findings

Much of the detail in this section is taken from the official Home Office Research Unit publication called "Community Service Orders," published in April 1975.

1. The Research Unit reported by July 1, 1974, that 1,172 orders had been made in the six experimental areas. At the time, 307 were satisfactorily completed, 114 unsatisfactorily terminated. Termination could be due to breach of the order or revocation.
2. The most common types of offenses for which community-service orders were made were as follows: property offenses—the majority, motoring offenses, offenses against the person, and miscellaneous.
3. Offenders on community service were drawn primarily from the 17-24-age range.
4. The average number of previous convictions of those ordered to undertake community service was three in some areas, four in the others.
5. Between 38 and 50 percent of offenders on community service had had experience of a custodial sentence.
6. It is shown that those with longer criminal records and those who had served a custodial sentence were less likely to terminate their order by completing it. The type of offense committed was not found to predict manner of an order's discharge.
7. Women were made subject of approximately 10 percent of all community-service orders.
8. Typically, a community-service order followed a probation officer's recommendation of that sentence. The courts' take-up rates of recommendation for community service varied between areas, but the average was probably not lower than that in relation to probation.
9. Not all community-service orders were made in cases where a custodial sentence would otherwise have been passed, but it is not possible to estimate at present with certainty the number that were.
10. Rates at which orders were made were sensitive to local difficulties and lack of publicity. Fluctuations in these rates are attributed more to fluctuations in number of probation officer recommendations of community service than to fluctuations in number of initiations of community-service consideration by courts.
11. The number of orders made differed between areas, but when corrected for the size of the probation areas, it seems that smaller schemes were not underdeveloped relative to the larger areas.

In Nottinghamshire, a small team of probation officers undertook some consumer research with offenders who had completed community-service orders. At the time of a colleague's report, 20 were interviewed successfully, 14 were unproductive, and six were awaited. There have been some interesting findings from the 20 successful interviews: 14 felt that they had served the community and only one of them did not think he had. All but two claimed that, knowing what they knew, they would still have agreed to community service. If this sentence had not existed, 13 felt that they would have received a custodial sentence, two a fine, and two probation or another sentence. Fifteen saw community service as an alternative to imprisonment; 17 felt that probation would have been of less benefit to them; and 17 felt that their community-service experience had been worthwhile. Only two of the 20 had been involved in community work before their sentence, but 12 were after their experience of community service, and these intended to continue with the work. An important aspect to emerge has been the development of the relationship between the offender and his supervisor, although no direct questions were asked about this. Of the 11 offenders who mentioned supervisors, nine spoke in very positive terms, and two in negative terms. One of the men interviewed said "the court order put me smack in the middle of where I always had wanted to be."

Dr. K. Pease of the Home Office Research Unit quoted his evaluation of the scheme as follows.

The community service experience shows that the scheme is viable. Orders are being made and completed, sometimes evidently to the benefit of the offenders concerned. However, the effect on the offenders as a whole is as yet unknown. The penal theory underlining the scheme is thought by some to be uncertain; it has not as yet made much impact on the prison population because of the manner of its use by the courts. In practice, a few supervisors may be able to subvert some orders of the court unless good contact at the work site is maintained by the probation service; and neither the type of offender for whom it is suitable, nor the most desirable work placement for different individuals on community service are as yet known. The writer feels much more optimistic about the scheme than the list implies, but has tried not to state the case for community service any more strongly than the evidence currently available justifies. It is intended to give a clearer picture of its outcome by examining the one year reconviction rate of offenders made subject to orders during the first year of the operation of the scheme in each of the experimental areas. At best, community service is an exciting departure from traditional penal treatment.

Future Directions

On August 1, 1974, the home secretary, having read the evidence to the home office research unit, announced the national extension of community-service schemes to all magistrates and crown courts in England and Wales. Probation areas outside the experimental projects were given approval to commence their own community-service schemes for April 1, 1975. To date, 95 percent of all probation areas in England and Wales have a partial or complete community-service scheme operative in their areas. The new areas are encouraged to set up community-service projects on a system of staggered development so that staff gain the necessary practice and expertise before enlarging the scheme to other parts of the area. Progress is also limited by cutbacks in government and local authority spending. However, despite these restrictions on growth, there is much optimism and interest in the scheme from both the probation staff and community organizations up and down the country.

As community service projects expand, the following implications seem to be of importance.

1. Some organizations who offer promising placements do not expand opportunities for offenders without some reallocation of staff time. This could often be at the expense of the growth of the organizations. If one is to maintain a range of placements with voluntary organizations, central government may have to consider grant aid to certain organizations willing to take offenders.

2. For some offenders, community service can involve a change of attitude, a different life style. This is particularly the case for offenders involved in personalized tasks. It would be dishonest to merely raise a young person's expectations without the hope of long-term fulfillment. Six ex-community-service offenders are currently employed as part-time supervisors in Nottinghamshire. Three more have gone off for training either in social work or youth work. But this is not enough. We must look for new opportunities and courses for offenders from the universities, colleges, hospitals, schools, and social work departments. Such a challenge will require additional funding and staff resources if the start made on community service is to be properly developed.

3. More research time is needed to investigate who is suitable for community service and what type of tasks are most appropriate.

4. The community-service experiments have been run by a specialist section of community-service staff. Although much has been done by the specialist staff, there is a need to centralize the organization of community service and involve local probation officers more closely in the scheme. One would therefore advocate a gradual move away from specialization to the point where each area team had its own staff member who was responsible for organizing community service from a local office. Colleagues could more readily share the responsibility for running the scheme and perhaps use its potential more fully. Such a transition has implications for those in charge of community-service training, and allowances should be made for this in terms of future planning.

5. Community service offers the probation service a real opportunity for partnership with community groups. In asking commmunity groups to accept and involve offenders as helpers, we are pushing back the conventional stereotypes of offenders and widening the threshold of tolerance. In that process, we are perhaps asking the community to grow with us, to share our success and failure, and make it more communicable.

Appendix 8A:
Case Illustration

Ann T.

Ann T. prefers to be called Colette W. Part of her difficulty lies in her wanting to be something else than herself. At times she wishes to detach herself from her previous identity and describes Ann T. as slow, clumsy, and rather conservative. She thinks that Collette W. fits in with a more sophisticated, confident image that she would like of herself.

Colette was adopted at the age of three months, and was raised by her parents in Hertfordshire. She was subsequently displaced by a younger natural child a year later. She says that "as she grew up her relationship with her mother deteriorated due to an inverted type of discrimination—in that her parents had never disciplined her in the same way that they had chastised Jenny." This pattern further emerges during her borstal training when she got the staff to collude sympathetically with her drug taking to the point where no control was exercised.

Colette's IQ is assessed at 140 and, although she only passed three '0' levels, it is clear that she has above-average intelligence. Much of her behavior over the last seven years has been of a familiar testing kind. She has tested her parents, rebelled against authority, and challenged people as a way of gaining recognition for herself. There have been several institutional periods during this time, including a probation home, probation hostel, borstal training, and a hospital for those suffering from a behavior disorder. Not surprisingly, her employment record is poor and patchy. She has worked as a stable maid and has had various odd jobs of short duration. She and her cohabitee, Jim Hughes, took an early discharge from the hospital in May 1972. They set up home with their baby in Nottingham. The relationship appears to have been both neurotic and destructive with the child as only means of holding them together. Eventually in frustration, both parents seem to have released their aggression on the child. Colette talks of guilt and is still very much self-obsessed. I found her insightful about herself, as one would expect, but lacking in ability to sustain a long-term relationship. She is very unsure of her identity, and sometimes wishes she were a man.

Colette is currently living on her own but will shortly change accommodation as she is being evicted from a council flat. There are plans for her to take a government training center course as a secretary in September. She is not particularly keen on this and even remarked that she preferred to take on a male trade like an electrician. She selected some tasks that would appeal to her, and again they reveal a certain identity with some of her own difficulties.

I feel community service could potentially be of immense value to this woman, although she may need a fairly protected start without too much demanding involvement. Her progress needs to be regularly assessed. It is useful to know that she already has a supervisor in Mrs. Brown.

Colette completed community service very satisfactorily. Most of her 200 hours were spent with the Family First Organisation, directed by Mrs. Smith. She performed a number of tasks for Mrs. Smith such as painting and decorating, gardening, clerical work, running a shop, etc.

Colette gained great support from the interest and concern which Family First show for all those involved with them, both staff and residents. It was an ideal placement. Mrs. Smith even attempted to sort out Colette's employment difficulties and arranged interviews for her with local colleges of education and the Department of Employment and Productivity. Colette in turn acknowledged her attachment to Mrs. Smith, and the more she became invested in the organization, the more satisfaction she obtained. We received no adverse reports about her, and the only complaint was that Colette overtaxed herself in terms of physical effort. She has a frail physique and is very prone to colds and chest complaints. Part of the difficulty is that she does not eat properly or dress warmly enough.

Colette also worked for the Rushbridge Luncheon Club and attended on 10 occasions. She helped prepare and serve meals for old aged pensioners. Once again progress was satisfactory, although I do not think Colette ever felt the same sense of involvement as with Family First.

Colette has expressed an interest in continuing to work for Family First, and this is to be encouraged. Her future is by no means clear, especially in terms of employment. The chief value of Family First is that Colette has begun to believe in herself again and has acquired the respect of other people.

Colin M.

Colin is 23 years old. He is of medium height, slightly overweight, and dresses casually but neatly. He has been married for just over a year and has a young child. He and his wife have lived on Crabtree Estate in Bulwell since their marriage. Colin is the youngest of the three children, both of the older ones being sisters. He feels that he gets on well with his family and is quite affectionate towards them. He was taken away from school at the age of 14 and was sent to Approved School because of continual truancy. This was his only other brush with the law. While at Approved School he obtained his first year city and guilds mechanics qualifications. He has now been working as a delivery driver for four years and is keen to own his own business (either a garage or in hairdressing supplies). His interests, he says, are limited to cars and football. Neither he nor his wife have many social activities. He was extremely pleasant during the inverview, and I felt that he was quite sharp and canny. He listed his priorities as:

1. Driving for old people's outings
2. Archaeological digs
3. Ambulance service (if driving)

We talked for some time about the first of these choices, and I suggested that it might be helpful if he linked up with a particular old people's home so that he already knew the people before taking them on outings. He seemed quite prepared to do this and suggested that his wife might also be interested. If she does join in with him on this, then it could have interesting repercussions on his continuing the work at the end of the order.

After my colleague's initial assessment of Colin, I arranged through an old contact with Joan Selby, the secretary of Basford Care Group, for him to be linked up with them on some of their Sunday excursions for old aged pensioners and handicapped people in the district. I also arranged from my contact with the University to borrow the community wagon from the students. As all this took a few weeks to arrange, in the interim period I arranged for Colin to do two jobs at Holme Pierrepont acting as a car marshall. It is interesting to note that although we had little success in terms of placement at the National Water Sports Centre, Colin and his friend Alan were two successes, so much so that the secretary forgot they were on community service and offered them both payment at the end of each occasion. Colin and Alan had to remind him that they were on community service! This pattern of total cooperation and concern has continued throughout Colin's order.

What happened with the Basford Care Group and the outings on Saturdays and Sundays throughout the summer and autumn has done nothing but credit to the scheme and to Colin Marshall himself. His initiative, kindness, and total willingness at every aspect of the Basford Care Group has impressed the organizers, the beneficiaries and the general public. I have always felt that Colin represented the best aspects of community service available for the total benefits of the scheme. Because of my feelings about this particular situation and the involvement with such a good voluntary group, he has been interviewed by the *Observor* newspaper, *The Evening Post*, and latterly his work has been filmed for BBC "Man Alive." The problem doesn't just end with Colin himself; his next door neighbor is Alan, also on community service, who is currently placed with the Eastville Youth Group under the guidance of Keith Ingram and Peter Lewis, both probation officers. However, Alan goes voluntarily as a driver/assistant bringing his own car on some of the outings. Colin's wife is also a valued member of the group, and they bring along their child with them. Just before Christmas the Care Group held a small party and gave presents to Colin and his wife by way of recognition of their efforts. They also managed to link up a 14-year-old probationer who had expressed interest in community service with Colin. He sits alongside him in the ambulance and acts as Colin's assistant.

Fortunately, the impressions of the Basford Care Group about Colin's work are excellently recorded by Joan Selby, and they form part of the record in this file. The evidence speaks for itself. It is interesting to note that halfway through the order, Colin tore up his record card and said he wasn't interested in the formality of the order itself. If Joan wanted him to help with the Care Group, he would come along willingly any time. The strength of this remark is revealed at the end of the order, when I understand he has now put in for a house transfer from Bulwell to be nearer the Care Group at Basford. His work with the Care Group has also caused one influential City Councillor, Jess Burton, to change his mind about community service by offenders. At the last annual general meeting of the Care Group in January, he made a public statement admitting he had judged the scheme too hastily and claimed his mind had been changed by Colin and his friends in their efforts for the work of the Care Group itself. Despite all the publicity that Colin has received, he has remained unruffled and cooperative throughout.

Peter C.

Peter is a member of a delinquent family well known to the probation service, and at the age of 25 had already experienced most sentences available to the courts, including Approved School, Detention Centre, Borstal Training, and two prison sentences. Social standards and control in the family home are reported as very low, while Peter's response to the various forms of institutional training he had undergone was described as promising. He had, in particular, taken an active part in community-based projects while in borstal. His record of convictions contained a preponderance of burglary and theft offenses, and joint or group offenses were also a common feature.

His community-service order was imposed by the Crown Court for offenses of theft and deception, the order being for the maximum of 240 hours. Although Peter had by this time enjoyed an apparently stable marriage for three years, the social inquiry report makes the following significant comment: "It is clear that he retains a strong emotional bond with his own family and this is reflected in the degree of his social and criminal involvement with his relatives. . . ." His employment record was reasonably good.

Peter's attitude at assessment was friendly and cooperative, but his motivation for community service seemed to derive mainly from his relief at being at liberty. He felt he was most suited to practical work but also expressed interest in helping at weekend youth camps, having some experience of camping himself. Initially, he was placed for general practical tasks at a group of bungalows for the elderly, and supervised by the resident warden. His first few weeks' work received good reports, but as the winter drew in, his attendance became more erratic. This was seen as due partly to his reluctance to undertake outdoor work such as gardening during the winter; but the fact that he was working alone rather than with a group of workers was also believed to be significant. He was therefore relocated with a group who were renovating a house for use as a halfway hostel for patients discharged from a local mental hospital. His response was good, and there was some evidence that he was beginning to develop some awareness of the needs of others, and a sense of responsibility for the work he was undertaking. He continued to attend in spite of domestic crises, notably his wife's deserting him and the loss of his job, and while not absolutely regular, his persistence at a time of crisis could be seen as surprising in a young man of his background.

The evidence of growing motivation and awareness in Peter was sufficiently strong at this point to justify his placement at a week's camp for handicapped adults arranged by the local social services department, which took place in a holiday area some distance away. The community worker responsible for the camp reported that he took a leading role in the success of the expedition. Unfortunately, however, during the week that he was away it emerged that he was suspected of involvement in a further joint burglary offense as having received stolen property. It was necessary for the police to arrest him at the camp, although this was undertaken with considerable discretion so as not to cause disruption to the other campers. Following his release on bail, he completed his order with a further weekend expedition of a group of offenders to the Derbyshire Peak Park, helping with a nature conservation project.

At the subsequent court appearance, a report on Peter's progress while on community service indicated that the order could be seen as extremely successful, with both Peter and the community having derived considerable benefit. In passing sentence, the judge indicated that this report of success had been a major factor in his deliberations and, in spite of Peter's bad record of offending, a suspended sentence of imprisonment was imposed.

Peter has remained in contact with his community service officer and has indicated his willingness to help as a volunteer on any project in his home area. Peter was one of the offenders subject to community service whose reoffending caused us most concern since it had appeared that a genuine change in his attitude to others was taking place as a result of his work for the elderly and handicapped. He and several others with a similar history led us to the tentative conclusion that extensively delinquent cultural influences, especially where these are strongly rooted in an offender's family of origin, may so dominate that the beneficial possibilities of community service cannot prevail.

David D.

At the age of 18, David's criminal record was relatively minor, but the offenses for which he appeared before the Crown Court were not. The prosecution described him as an experienced housebreaker who had become a great nuisance to householders and indicated that although he was considerably younger than his codefendant, there was nothing to choose between them in terms of criminal sophistication. Three of the offenses were of burglary with intent (throwing a brick through a bank window and being found on the premises). He asked for fourteen other offenses to be taken into consideration. His codefendant had been dealt with at an earlier date by way of a suspended prison sentence, and the judge indicated that this was the main reason why David had avoided a Borstal sentence and had instead attracted the 150-hour community-service order which had been guardedly recommended in the social inquiry report.

David's childhood history was disrupted, first by his contracting diabetes at the age of 5 years, as a consequence of which he spent four years during childhood receiving in-patient hospital treatment because of difficulties in stabilizing his condition. He spent regular holidays at home, however, and apparently detected that his parents' marriage was failing. His absconding and difficult behavior compelled his discharge from in-patient treatment at the age of 11, but the emotional pressures within the family provoked the continuation of such behavior by David and, after considerable truancy and delinquency which two years of supervision could not influence, he was committed to the care of the local authority. He returned to his mother's home after his parents had separated, but his employment record developed a pattern of serious inconsistency.

During pretrial inquiries, David had shown some resistance to the idea of further probation supervision, and such a recommendation would probably have been unrealistic in view of the gravity of the offenses. However, comments he made during the assessment interview and his subsequent behavior suggest the possibility that he had a need for personal support and guidance, and that in various ways he sought this from community service. He at first showed some understandable interest in working as a helper in a children's home, but detailed discussion elicited rather authoritarian attitudes about the best way to handle children with difficult behavior. These comments, and his general immaturity, indicated that it would be unwise to risk such a placement. However, it is also possible to speculate that David's remarks contained some reference to his own difficult behavior as a child and later, and some element of need for control and punishment. Other references he made to an interest in joining an army cadet corps appear to support this. He accepted the suggestion that he join practical work groups in the first instance and was allocated to painting and decorating.

His attendance was exceptionally good, and he completed the order in three months, usually working both Saturdays and Sundays. Early in the order the opportunity arose for David to accompany a combined group of other community-service offenders and younger boys on probation on a weekend expedition to a National Trust property to assist with nature conservation work. Although quiet and diffident in group relationships, his work and behavior were good. However, painting and decorating groups appeared to meet his needs more accurately, particularly through the opportunity offered to develop a relationship with a supervisor. His first supervisor was a girl only a few years older than himself, who had particular abilities in gaining the trust and confidence of those as shy and withdrawn as David.

He discussed with her a number of problems not previously disclosed, including his fears of being a homosexual, and her positive influence led to his enrolling for evening classes in order to take "0" level examinations. However, she herself felt that he began to overidentify with her, and his past difficulties with his father suggested that the experience of male supervision might be of value to him. This was achieved without difficulty when two groups were working together and a male supervisor, himself an exoffender, was able to interest David in changing groups. Although this occurred at a time when David had nearly completed the hours laid down by the court, he continued to work with the group as a reliable volunteer for some months afterwards. David sought much advice and guidance from this supervisor and came to hold great respect for him. Perhaps an even clearer sign of the extent to which David had begun to mature was his ability to integrate himself among his peers in the work group.

The history of David's community-service order demonstrates the potential of this method in offering new solutions to problems that had proved insoluble by other methods at other periods in his life. Direct intervention into the family's problems had been thoroughly attempted but without much success, and he had already indicated his own reluctance to receive further casework help. However, his disrupted history and family relationships had clearly left him with a major employment problem and a need for control and firm guidance. Never having resolved problems in parental relationships, he had not even begun to make satisfactory peer-group relationships.

Although it would be foolish to make predictions about the extent to which David may have been influenced against further offending, his story also illustrates some of the special rewards of this method for the workers and supervisors involved. There are aspects of David's progress on community service that can be identified very clearly. His near-perfect record of attendance is no matter of speculation, but an objective fact, and as gratifying to the community-service staff as it perhaps is to David himself. His practical work and response to supervisors contrasts sharply with his past employment history. While David's community-service order was clearly imposed as a direct alternative to a probable custodial sentence, it became a medium for indirect and very practical intervention in some of the areas in which he had "treatment" needs.

Appendix 8B:
Task List

Personal Help

Youth
Helping at youth clubs, organizing sports and discos, running coffee bars.

Helping to run weekend camps and expeditions.

Helping to run a junior football team.

Children
Helping in a residential children's home.

Helping to run a preschool play group or holiday play scheme.

Handicapped
Helping with swimming clubs, sports clubs, riding for the disabled, holiday play schemes.

Helping at social clubs for the handicapped of all ages.

Helping at a school for mentally handicapped children.

Helping as a driver for club meetings or day outings.

Helping with a shopping service for the disabled at Victoria Centre.

Helping with activities for mentally handicapped hospital patients.

Elderly
Helping in an old people's home.

Helping at an old people's day center or club with activities, catering, transport, and outings.

Practical Help

Building
Renovation and construction work on projects for the homeless, children's play schemes, community centers, adventure playgrounds, clubs for the handicapped, projects of historical interest. All building and practical skills welcome.

Painting and Decorating
Painting and decorating work for the elderly, handicapped, fatherless families, various community projects.

Countryside and Gardening	Helping at National Trust parks to improve the countryside—forestry, drainage and clearance work, etc.

Countryside and Gardening Helping at National Trust parks to improve the countryside—forestry, drainage and clearance work, etc.

Helping a footpath preservation society.

Helping a canal preservation society.

Gardening for handicapped, elderly, and for community projects, associations, etc.

Workshop Helping with the renovation and setting-up of the workshop.

Helping in the workshop with toy making and repair, furniture making and repair, equipment for youth clubs, conversion of equipment for the handicapped, etc.

Motor maintenance and repair of vehicles belonging to community groups.

General

Helping at a neighborhood advice center, tenants' association or housing association, or with a community newspaper—general, clerical, practical help or advice.

Help at a soup kitchen or night shelter for vagrants and the homeless.

Helping at a club for isolated single people, exprisoners, etc.

Helping to collect and deliver furniture for needy families.

Helping at charity events—fetes etc.

Transport Numerous opportunities for qualified drivers with clean driving licenses, especially those with PSV licenses or those with their own properly insured vehicles.

Other Opportunities If you have any other worthwhile activity to suggest, or some special interest, skill, or hobby, don't hesitate to mention it.

Implementing Restitution Within a Penal Setting: The Case for the Self-determinate Sentence

Kathleen D. Smith

The type of restitution I wish to suggest is direct payment in money by offenders to their victims. I believe it is possible to combine the payment of monetary restitution with every form of treatment now being used for physically and mentally fit offenders who have reached the legal minimum age for full-time employment; and that the success rates of all treatments would be improved by the combination. But an essential prerequisite to restitution is a sanction that ensures that offenders cannot default in making payments. The ultimate sanction are prisons equipped as factories, in which inmates work full time, receive full union rates of pay for all work done, and are obliged to use most of their earnings to compensate their victims. Such prisons would be the immediate home for major or persistent offenders and the ultimate destination for other offenders who were permitted, but failed, to pay restitution in noncustodial surroundings.

The benefits of introducing direct restitution from offenders to victims are manifold: It would demonstrably bring better justice to victims, who now understandably feel bewildered and indignant as the rights of offenders are meticulously considered and protected by the courts, while the rights of victims seem hardly to exist. Improved justice for victims would in turn improve the relationship between the public and the offender: A law-breaker who paid for his crime in cash would be far less stigmatized, far more acceptable, than one who merely undergoes treatment as a nonpaying guest of the nation. Equally important, the self-esteem of offenders would improve as they paid their way back to equality in society. Above all, the incidence of crime would be diminished by the requirement of restitution—crime would not be nearly so attractive a proposition if criminals, when caught, had to pay back every penny of damage done and gains illegally acquired.

Since leaving the British Prison Service in 1960 convinced of the efficacy of restitution as a curb to the crime wave, I have been campaigning in Britain through the media and politics to get the benefits of restitution understood and implemented. By 1968 the Conservative Party had accepted the principle of restitution and in its manifesto of 1970 declared that, if returned to government, it would "change the law so that the criminal who causes personal injury or damages property will be obliged to compensate his victim in addition to other punishments imposed by the Courts."

Having won the General Election of 1970, the Conservatives produced the Criminal Justice Act 1972, which permits magistrates' courts to order offenders to pay up to £400 (just over $800) in compensation for each offense committed and allows the crown courts to order limitless compensation and to declare bankrupt those offenders involved in crimes valued at over £15,000 ($30,000) and to use their assets to compensate their victims.

Unfortunately, in practice these provisions are not so forceful as they appear on paper, for the courts are directed to have regard to an offender's means before making a compensation order against him. If he has money, the court proceeds to make him pay, or if he has a job, compensation can be deducted in installments from his wages. However, if he is unemployed with no visible means of support other than social security benefits—and these are the circumstances of most persistent offenders—then the courts refrain from making compensation orders since there is no way an offender without resources can be obliged to pay. The ability of the crown courts to declare major offenders bankrupt is similarly an abortive provision since major criminals are usually astute enough not to have any property in their own name. Consequently, to declare them bankrupt produces nothing. The only remedy left to the courts is to send them to prison—where it currently costs £60 ($120) weekly to keep them; where the average inmate is employed for 24 hours and many for fewer than 20 hours each week, for which they receive wages averaging about 80 pence ($1.60) weekly; and where the pace of their work may be calculated from the fact that they produce on average a mere £8 ($16) of goods each a week.

The moral of this situation is that until we have prisons that oblige offenders to work to pay through their earnings the restitution they owe, law-breakers—particularly the professionals—will continue to avoid compensation orders and welcome jail as an easy option.

There are, of course, both complications and objections to turning prisons into workshops for restitution. In Britain the main complication comes from the two lines of thought about prison reform that emanate from the home office.

One of these can best be illustrated by an eight-year and £14 million ($28 million) project, now half completed, at Her Majesty's Prison, Holloway, London: the largest women's prison in the United Kingdom. The Victorian edifice, opened in 1852, is being demolished, and in its place is rising a new prison, the design of which is to be the prototype of future men's prisons. Officially described as "a medically oriented establishment with a comprehensive, versatile and secure hospital as its central feature," the New Holloway will have an operating theater manned by visiting surgeons; a psychodiagnostic unit caring for disturbed inmates and those in the withdrawal stages of alcoholics, and disturbed women; an obstetric unit giving pre- and postnatal care; a unit for mothers wishing to have the company of their children up to the age of 5; another unit for illiterate prisoners who will have daily specialist teaching; and one for remand prisoners who are also first offenders who will be segregated from other prisoners. Women not requiring any of the special-care units will have the services of a psychotherapist, will be part of a psychotherapeutic community, and will join in an hour-and-a-half of group counseling each week.

In addition to the leisure aids available in the old Holloway—radio, television, games, and evening classes—women in the new prison will have the use of a swimming pool, a gymnasium, and a hairdressing salon. Another innovation will be a dress boutique where they will be able to buy clothes for wearing when they leave prison or during their sentence.

When I wrote an article on the new Holloway for the *Daily Telegraph* in 1972, two years after the project was begun, I was impressed by the detailed consideration that had been given to the ways in which the prison would care for the women, and wondered how much provision had been made for the ways in which the women could make a contribution to society. I asked what plans there were for the women's work. I was told by an official who was one of the leading inspirers of the design of the new Holloway that while a workshop was included in the prison, what work or working hours it would offer had not been decided. "What Holloway wants"—to quote this official—

is a Government contract for the sort of work for which there is an everlasting demand, which requires little skill, and which can be put down at any moment when prisoners are called away for treatment or legal matters. What I have been suggesting is that they should knit dishcloths. There must be an endless need of dishcloths in all the Government establishments throughout the country.

It struck me as tragic that the planners of the new Holloway had devoted so much attention to providing comforts, amusements, and treatments for all possible sickness and abnormalities of prisoners, while scarcely concerning themselves with outlets for the useful, responsible, constructive, and contributive activities of prisoners.

No one doubts the desirability and value of useful employment for nonprisoners. To prisoners, it is far more vital. An unemployed civilian has at least some of the other blessings of life—home, family, friends, freedom, decision. In addition, he always has the prospect of getting a job. A prisoner has only those prospects and actions that prison allows him. Every important attachment, choice possession of normal life, is reduced for him to a minimum. His family and friends are relegated to a controlled number of letters and visits. Wherever he goes, he is watched or thinks he is watched. Everything about him is subject to criticism, from the way he talks to the way he walks and cleans his shoes. If he is not permitted to displace his energies and frustrations in the satisfaction of work, there is a low probability of his recollecting enough of the habit, interest, and confidence of normal life to be able to fit into it again when the time comes. To expect him to do so is something worse than stupidity.

For these reasons, a work schedule should have been planned in as meticulous a manner as all the other amenities in the new Holloway.

The second school of thought on prison reform that emanates from the home office is expressed in *The Report on the Work of the Prison Department, 1974*, which says that "there has been a move away from the medical model that persistent offending is a sickness susceptible to individual diagnosis, treatment and cure." Since 1969 this attitude has been applied in practice at Coldingley Prison, Surrey, where work is regarded as the main treatment. Up to 300 men work 40 hours a week in a fully modernized laundry or in workshops making steel shelving or signposts, for which they receive about £2 a week, which they can spend as they wish. In its five years of operation, Coldingley has had no serious trouble and has met its production targets. While this success shows that it is possible to incorporate into the prison system a full working week, it must be remembered that the population of Coldingley is less than 1 percent of the total British prison population of 40,000; that the inmates at Coldingley are carefully selected and are removed to other prisons if uncooperative; that it has been found difficult at times to motivate even these selected men to produce work to the standards required by outside industries; and that, so far, a study of reconviction indicates that there is no significant difference either in reconviction rate, or speed of reconviction, between Coldingley men and similar men in other prisons.

It is evident, then, that to persuade 100 percent of prisoners to work full time with full effort, to motivate them so that their work is consistently of an acceptable standard, and to have a beneficial effect on their reconviction rates is going to require more incentive than £2 per week. It is going to require the incentives of the self-determinate sentence: a 42-hour working week rewarded with full union rates of pay for all work completed to acceptable standards and the requirement for prisoners to remain in prison until by compensating their victims, they have paid for their crimes out of earnings.

I have called this system the "self-determinate sentence" because the length of sentence an offender serves under it is to be the greatest possible extent his own responsibility. It is determined *first* by the type of crime he commits, and *second* by the effort he makes during his sentence to compensate for his crime. It would apply equally to men and women.

While I shall mainly describe the effects of the self-determinate sentence on British courts and prisons, I think there are enough similarities with those of other nations to show that the principles are internationally applicable.

Instead of assessing offenses in terms of time to be served in custody, the courts would assess them in *money to be earned.* Offenses involving victims would be assessed in two ways: first by the restitution due to the victim for physical, material, and in cases of terrorization, for psychological damage sustained. I would suggest that psychological damage, which is often the most serious of harms suffered by victims, is at present too often disregarded by the courts and should have more consideration given to it in sentencing. Second, fines would be levied at the court's discretion in relation to the offender's persistence and intent.

The proceeds of fines would be directed into a *national compensation fund*, from which compensation would be paid to victims of offenders too sick physically or mentally or too old to work; or by those whose death took place subsequent to conviction. Offenses involving no victim—drunkeness, prostitution, drug-taking—would be subject to fines that would also be paid into the national compensation fund.

The courts would direct whether the whole or part of any fine or compensation should be paid from earnings in prison; and what part, if any, could be paid from private monies.

Crimes against property would be assessed according to the value of the property damaged or stolen, and stolen property voluntarily restored might, as the court directed, be deducted from the compensation ordered. This would not, however, provide an automatic discharge for offenders who restored all their ill-gotten gains. Few crimes can be so simply dismissed. If terrorization had been caused to the owner of the property because of the offense committed against his property, this would have to be compensated for and fines would be in force according to the record of the offender and the strength of the deterrent deemed necessary. Nevertheless, stolen property that was voluntarily restored would generally have the effect of reducing compensation. This would encourage the recovery of much stolen property: an incentive lacking in our present system of committal.

The machinery required for assessing compensation for victims of crimes of violence already exists in Britain. Since 1964 victims of assaults have been able to apply to the Criminal Injuries Compensation Board for reparation. The Board has paid out £19 million since its inauguration and now receives upwards of 12,000 claims a year, 85 percent of which result in monetary awards. No compensation is paid for damages valued at less than £50. Ninety-nine percent of victims receive less than £5,000. The highest award made so far has been £55,000. These awards are paid out of the National Exchequer. Although it is possible to sue assailants in the civil courts to recover damages for personal injuries, the Criminal Injuries Compensation Board have estimated that in less than 1 percent of the cases they resolve is there an identified offender worth suing. So the most that is required of the vast majority of attackers is that they spend a useless term in prison.

While it is laudable that victims of violence now receive compensation for the damage done to them, it is heinous that assailants are not required to pay for the injuries. If they were obliged to compensate for the harm they inflicted through the self-determinate sentence, it is reasonable to predict that crimes of violence would be far less frequently resorted to.

Under the self-determinate sentence the compensation due for murder or manslaughter would vary, not according to the value of the life taken—for who can assess that?—but according to the motive, provocation, and method of the killing. For instance, a killing in which the motive was one of releasing a person from suffering is less culpable, and would attract less compensation, than a murder committed in order to obtain the victim's property. Similarly, there are exonerating degrees of provocation: Some murders are committed under provocation of such intensity and duration that the victim of the killing becomes almost as responsible for the killing as the assailant himself. Murder provoked by a personal relationship is more excusable than one committed on a passer-by whom the criminal regarded as an obstruction or as fortuitous prey. As to method, homicide with an instrument picked up in the heat of the moment is less to be condemned than, for instance, murder by systematic poisoning over a period of time.

Instead of the deadly, irredeemable practice of executing a killer—a practice which, in fact, a substantial majority of people in Britain would like to see restored—or of assessing murder by the number of years a murderer shall be confined in prison before atonement is presumed complete, the self-determinate sentence would require all killers to make it a major part of their life's work to compensate, as far as is possible, the dependents of their victims. In the case of a victim with no dependents or of a victim with dependents unwilling to accept compensation, the compensation due would be paid into the national compensation fund.

Except in exceptional circumstances—for example, the natural death of a person concerned in committing a crime—the whole of the compensation due to the victim of any crime would be payable in full by the person or persons convicted of that crime, even though it was known that other people were involved in committing it. This would induce convicted offenders to name their confederates, assist the police in making arrests, deter gang crimes, and break up the solidarity of the underworld.

Compensation would not necessarily be ordered to be paid equally by all accomplices. The courts would order the proportion to be paid by each according to the available evidence as to the degree of participation and anticipated gain of each offender. Likewise, fines would not necessarily be imposed equally on all offenders.

Offenders who volunteered information leading to the conviction of others might, at the court's discretion, have the whole or part of the compensation ordered against them made payable by the national compensation fund. Fines imposed might be waived in whole or in part for the same reason. These acts of leniency would be an additional incentive for offenders to name their accomplices.

Before any compensation or fine could be paid from his earnings, each prisoner would be required to make the appropriate contribution toward his pension and health benefits, to pay income tax, and to contribute towards his keep in prison. A sum of £5 a week would cover food and clothing in British prisons. The act of paying for basic keep would have the favorable side-effect of inducing prisoners to request that it should remain simple, rather than to clamour for it to be made increasingly elaborate.

Compulsory savings of £25 ($50) would also be deducted from prisoners' wages for their use on discharge. This sum, added to the social security benefits already paid to prisoners on their release, would add to their sense of freedom and security and would reduce, or at least postpone, the temptation to re-embark on a life of crime in order to maintain themselves. Furthermore, it would give them an opportunity to get decent lodgings if they had no home of their own. Too often, for lack of funds, the homeless exprisoner lands up at a hostel full of other exprisoners—which is not the most favorable circumstance for beginning a law-abiding life.

Pocket-money for use in prison would be allowed as 5 percent of earnings after the basic charges for National Insurance, income tax, keep, and compulsory savings had been met. The salaries of prison staff and the cost of maintaining prisons—the two chief items of prison expenditure—would not be made a charge on prisoners' earnings but would continue to be financed out of public money as public services.

A large proportion of people in prison are not guilty, or have not been found guilty, of criminal offenses. The self-determinate sentence would be modified to suit their circumstances. The largest group of these are on remand awaiting trial. They would be allowed full-time, fully paid work during their remand period, or, as now, would be free to devote all or part of their time to preparing their case. Their earnings, after the basic deductions, would be their own property to use as they wished. Should a remand prisoner not be convicted at trial, any payment made for board and lodging while in prison would be refunded.

Remand prisoners convicted on trial and waiting in prison for sentence would receive no refund of payments made for their keep in prison, whether they finally received a sentence of imprisonment or not. Money earned by prisoners after conviction and while awaiting sentence, which exceeded the amount needed for basic deductions, would be saved for the prisoner either for his use on release, in the event of his not receiving a prison sentence, or for use towards compensation or fines, in the event of his being sentenced to imprisonment.

In addition to criminal cases, British prisons house civil prisoners. These are mainly imprisoned for refusal to pay income tax, National Insurance contributions, or wife and child maintenance. Under the self-determinate prison sentence, they would remain in prison until their debts had been paid. Other civil prisoners are committed to custody because of contempt of court, and remain in prison for unspecified periods until the court considers that their contempt has been purged. The dignity of the courts and the majesty of the law must obviously be upheld, but to sentence a person sine die in order to appease a court too often causes suffering quite out of proportion to the person's offense. It is a distressing, oppressive, and archaic sentence which can cause cruel mental suffering by coercing those merely guilty of speaking their mind, or of acting according to their own concept of justice, into apologizing for and retracting what they consider right. The self-determinate sentence would provide for a maximum fine to be imposed on those committing contempt of court, which fine would be reimposed if the contempt recurred.

Prisoners detained for deportation would be liable to pay compensation and fines if found guilty of an offense in the country deporting them. However, if deportation was being carried out at the request of another country, these prisoners would not be subject to the self-determinate sentence. They would, however, be given the opportunity of working and earning.

Prisoners appealing against conviction or sentence would be granted time from work to prepare their case. No wages would be paid in respect to this free time, but the prisoner would be responsible for paying basic charges. However, prisoners acquitted upon appeal would have refunded the total sum paid for prison keep, compensation and fines, since the date of their first committal to prison for the offense in question. A victim of crime who had received compensation for the crime committed against him would not be required to refund the compensation, even though the offender originally convicted of the offense was subsequently acquitted. Compensation arising from this contingency would be the liability of the national compensation fund.

The compensation for all offenses would be ordered and paid in the form of a lump sum, not as a series of installments. The lump sum would be paid to the victim by the national compensation fund immediately on the sentence of the offender. It would then devolve upon the prison authorities to recover this sum from the offender by means of his work for the reimbursement of the fund.

Upon medical advice to a court of an offender's inability to work because of senility or chronic physical or mental illness, the court would be empowered to impose a term of imprisonment instead of a sum of compensation on the offender. Similarly, should a prisoner's health seriously deteriorate during a self-determinate sentence rendering him incapable of work for a prolonged period, it would be possible for his sentence to be reviewed and converted to a timed sentence. Such provisions would be small invitation to malingering. Senility and the more malignant diseases are hard to fake, and not worth the agony of trying.

The compensation due from chronically sick or senile offenders would be paid out of the national compensation fund. Should an offender regarded as chronically sick recover sufficiently during his sentence to resume work, facilities would be provided for him to do so. Any money he earned above that required for basic deductions would be paid into the fund.

The amount of compensation and fines due would not be affected by prisoners' temporary sickness. They would be required to resume the payment of these after their recovery. Temporary illness does not excuse civilians from their liabilities (on the contrary, it often increases them); nor would it excuse prisoners from theirs. During their sickness they would, however, receive the sick pay to which civilian workers are entitled and this would cover basic deductions and make a small contribution toward compensation or fines due.

In order to give further incentive to sustained effort as well as an opportunity for a more normal life for all prisoners, two weeks' vacation with pay would be awarded for the completion of 50 weeks (not necessarily consecutive) of satisfactory work. This right would be granted for reasons that vacations are granted to every working person: for health, as a reward for work done, as a recharge for future effort.

Prisoners completing their sentence before becoming eligible for an annual vacation, would be paid on release the proportionate vacation pay which is due. The vacation pay of each inmate would be based on his average earnings during the past 50 weeks. The days during which a prisoner was sick would count towards the 50 weeks qualifying him for a vacation. The days during which he was absent from work through idleness, offense or escape, would not count toward this qualification.

Suitable prisoners would be allowed out of prison for their vacation. For others there would be a rest prison, maintained for vacation purposes. Extensive visits would be allowed from family and friends, comforts would be more liberal, food less plain, entertainments and sports freely organized, and alcohol available. The tariff for this fare would naturally be somewhat higher than that charged for keep in a working prison. If he so wished, a prisoner could continue to work instead of taking an annual vacation, thus enabling him to hasten his release, should he choose to devote his vacation pay to the sum of money outstanding against him.

As an extra incentive to sustain prisoners in their work, parole might be granted to those not regarded as a menace to public safety, when three-quarters of their restitution had been paid, so that they might make the final quarter of their payment from work in civilian life. If parolees failed to maintain regular payments they would be returned to prison.

The self-determinate sentence makes work as attractive as possible to prisoners. The overriding factor that would persuade most prisoners to make an effort would be that on their work would depend their pay, and on their pay would depend their release date. Few would consider it worthwhile to sabotage a system that settles the length of their sentence in their own hands.

Moreover, this system would give the greatest possible encouragement to offenders not to offend again as well as to potential offenders not to offend at all, for it would reduce the value of crime as an investment. At present major robberies represent a very good investment: the larger the robbery, the more it is worth the risk of the criminal having to wait a few years in prison before enjoying the proceeds. The offender obviously counts on not being caught, but he also reckons that being caught is not so important provided that the loot is big enough and he has held it long enough to get it stored away safely for future use. Prison lounging becomes a well-paid occupation in these circumstances. The self-determinate sentence would offer no such bargain. There would be very little attraction in salting away a stolen fortune for enjoyment after sentence if the sentence consisted of working until the fortune was restored.

The self-determinate sentence would provide persistent petty offenders with practice in regular work, which would aid them in returning to civilian life and confer on them the dignity of at least paying their way while in custody. Some recidivists become incapable of making a satisfactory life outside of prison. Prison is the place best known to them, where their friends are, and provision and order and guidance and no worry. These people are not professional criminals. The only hope of gain from their crimes they can possibly have is the privilege of living in an institution. They nearly all commit crimes against property, and if the total value of all their offenses were added up and divided by their sentences, it would reckon out at a handful of pounds worth of crime for every year spent in jail. By means of the self-determinate sentence, their offenses would be paid for in a matter of weeks. This fact may cause some to object that the self-determinate sentence would release persistent petty offenders frequently, thus causing society and the police the nuisance of more minor crimes and the expense of more detection and trials. But society has no moral right to imprison people for years for the sake of a few pounds' worth of goods. However, much as some offenders may need prison as a haven, and repeatedly return there, we are not justified in prejudging their actions and prejudicing their future by detaining them in prison for longer than is merited by the actual offenses they have committed.

The most beneficial effect of the self-determinate sentence is likely to be felt by those undergoing their first prison sentence. The encouragement of their ability as wage-earners and their restoration to respectability by their own efforts would fit them both psychologically and practically to renounce crime—and in so far as first-time prisoners are persuaded from crime, the unhappier problem of recidivist offenders is diminished.

In order to change the present prison system to that of the self-determinate sentence the practical considerations are: the types of industries most suitable, the finance required to establish them, the effect of the system on prison routine, and the means by which the self-determinate system shall gradually be introduced into the present system.

Initially, the type of industries required are those that offer productive work that can be learned in a few hours so that from the beginning of his sentence every able prisoner is fully and gainfully employed. Such jobs are often repetitive and dull; they are also essential, commercial, and remunerative. Such jobs are also endured by millions of law-abiding workers throughout the world as a means of making a living. Assembly work, press work and production-line work on components for the car industry, for electrical and household appliances, and for the furniture trade could provide such jobs. Equipment for government departments, which provides the main source of employment for prisoners at present, could continue to be manufactured, but under the self-determinate sentence this work would need to be highly organized, highly productive, guaranteed as to standards and delivery, and costed and paid for at commercial rates.

Once these types of industries had been established in several prisons, a more adventurous approach to the provision of work could be considered in order to extend the skills of the more able prisoners. Nor would work then be confined entirely within the prison precincts. The formation of working parties for road construction, building, forestry, farming and land reclamation would be encouraged.

In the prison factories, as in outside factories, there would be scope not only for production workers, but for the talents of clerks, cleaners, typists, cooks, canteen staff, maintenance workers, laborers, packers—enough for most ages and abilities. The wages of nonproductive workers would be based on the overall average wages of productive workers, to ensure that prisoners with comparable amounts of compensation ordered against them would have comparable opportunities of earning their release. However, in order that high average wage rates were maintained, it would be necessary that production workers should enjoy the incentives of piece-work rates and group-bonus schemes, which would mean that some might earn considerably more than others. It might be argued that this would cause unfair discrepancies in wages and the consequent ability to purchase freedom. There are three counterarguments to this: first, that income tax would somewhat reduce the effective amount that high earners received; second, that the opportunity to reach top wages would be equal for all; third, that high wages for production workers would benefit nonproduction workers since the wages of the latter would be based on the average of the former.

It would not be part of self-determinate sentence policy to submit prisoners to lengthy trade training during their working hours. The wages of apprenticeship would be neither adequate nor attractive to people trying to earn their way out of custody. However, voluntary evening and weekend trade training schemes would be available.

In order to allow for adjustment and experiment during the initial stages of the industrialization of prisons, prison factories would be financed by the government. Subsequently, as the scheme expanded, private firms might well be found willing to put up factories to their own requirements and to employ prisoners exactly as they would employ civilian workers—leaving discipline of prisoners to prison staff. Alternatively, the government might provide factory buildings and rent them to firms that would install the plant.

Fortunately, in Britain at least, there would be no expense or problem in acquiring suitable sites for factories, for there are ample grounds within the precincts of prisons, both in rural and urban areas. Most existing workshops would also be suitable for adaptation.

The chief effect of the self-determinate sentence on prison routine is that work would take priority over all other activities. At present, the loopholes allowed to prisoners to escape from what work they have are liberal and inviting. Interviews with the governor and consultations with the doctor are available daily on application and take place during working time. Queueing for these interviews usually take longer than the interviews themselves, and this time waste and chance for gossip are frequently the only real reasons for prisoners visiting these officials. Baths, attendance at clinics, sessions with psychiatrists, and visits from loved ones and solicitors are also enjoyed during working hours. As wages are not docked—except in the few cases where work is paid for at piece rates—for absenteeism on these excursions, prisoners are encouraged to exploit them. This would be changed so that interviews and visits would take place outside of working hours, except that remands and appellants would be allowed time off work for legal preparations, and emergency medical treatment would be given immediately. Otherwise, prisoners wishing to consult a doctor would do so at evening surgery, as working people do outside prison. Similarly, psychiatric treatment would also be given during inmates' leisure time. It is quite usual for civilians to combine a full working life with psychiatric treatment. Many psychiatrists consider a full working life helpful to such treatment.

The self-determinate sentence would not circumscribe any treatment or amenity now available to a prisoner. Making them available to him only during his own time, however, would end false demands on them. Inmates would no longer use them because they were work-avoiders, but only if they were of intrinsic value to them. Some types of activity now fairly well supported might disappear completely: some evening classes, for instance, might die under the influence of prisoners' time becoming more precious to them. The wish for new activities, advanced skills, adult information, might well emerge from the circumstance of prisoners becoming wage-earning, bill-paying people.

The rearrangement of routine and its expansion to provide a fuller life for prisoners would require some change in the training of staff and the work required of them. Certain officers would hold the position of foremen or inspectors in the workshops, remaining on duty during the prisoners' working hours. Others would cover leisure time, conducting visits, arranging interviews, supervising sports, hobbies, classes, and the prison shop, and staffing the rest prison used for prisoners' vacations.

The busy normal-as-possible life would require that fewer hours be spent locked in cells. The evening locking-up time would be deferred as soon as possible to 10 p.m. At present, at the commencement of a sentence it is 4:30 p.m. In many prisons, raised to 7 p.m. or 8 p.m. after some weeks.

Despite the extra hours of activity the self-determinate sentence would afford to prisoners, it would not necessarily need a larger staff to implement it than does the existing routine, for it would economize on staff in two ways: first, organizing prisoners' work in large groups in factories, whereas now it is not uncommon for an officer to be in charge of only one or two prisoners in a working party, and frequently to be in charge of half a dozen or fewer; second, by banning the interruption of work by the coming and going of prisoners to and from interviews, which is now part of the staff-consuming regime.

As prisoners' lives become more adult, so would punishments for their misconduct in prison. These would be self-determinate, like the sentence, and would take the form of fines to be paid out of earnings. This would have the effect of reducing pocket-money in the case of minor offenses, and of delaying release and/or eligibility for vacations in the case of more serious offenses.

Refusal to work or idleness would result in the offender being dismissed from work and confined to his cell for the day of his offense, and not permitted to resume work until the following day, which would have the effect of postponing his release and/or vacation by the loss of earning time he had brought on himself. It is difficult to imagine a prisoner condemning himself to prolonged solitary confinement by persistently refusing to work, but anyone who wished would be free to do so. His liabilities would accrue during his absence from labor, to await him when he chose to resume responsible activities. Prolonged refusal to cooperate might indicate an abnormal mental state and would always be accompanied by strict observation of the inmate's mental condition, which might lead, in some cases, to the certification of the prisoner as mentally unfit and his removal to a psychiatric hospital, where he would no longer be subject to the self-determinate sentence.

The introduction of the self-determinate sentence into the penal system would need to be gradual. Ideally, it would be pioneered in a prison equipped to employ about 1,000 prisoners, but beginning with a group of about 300, so that settling-in adjustments could be made easily as the population expanded. There would be two methods of selecting the pioneer group of prisoners: first, long-term prisoners—those with sentences of 4 years and upwards, including life sentences—would be allowed to appeal to be resentenced under the conditions of the self-determinate sentence. From boredom and curiosity, from a genuine desire to work and save money, from the hope of parole, from the attraction of a vacation, and because of the possibility of ending up with a shorter sentence, hundreds of offenders would take this opportunity. Many, however, would not: because of the brief time of their sentence remaining, because of their institutionalization, because of their dislike for work and the thought of paying restitution.

It would be made clear to prisoners that the proportion of their original sentence that had already been served would be taken into consideration when resentencing them so that only partial compensation and fines would be levied against them.

The remainder of the prisoners pioneering the self-determinate sentence would not be volunteers. They would be those generally considered most difficult: those sentenced for crimes of violence. After a given date the courts would sentence all these offenders to the self-determinate sentence. They would be chosen as the first to be compulsorily sentenced to the new system because, unlike the volunteer group of prisoners, they would be likely to provide a difficult test for it and also because the machinery for assessing restitution for crimes of violence already exists in the Criminal Compensation Board. Thereafter, as more prisons were industrialized, dates would be set from which the courts would apply the self-determinate sentence to all categories of offense. It would be last applied to offenses which involve no victim. In five years the changeover to the new system would be complete.

An important side-effect of the system would be that sentences would fit offenses more predictably and intelligibly, and the disparity of sentences now being passed by different courts for similar crimes, which causes so much indignation and misunderstanding about justice, would be minimized, and where it seemed apparent could more readily be challenged.

Here, I would like to make clear that although throughout this paper I have referred to the effect of the self-determinate sentence on prisons, it would apply not only to establishments devoted to adult offenders, but to custodial institutions for the treatment of young offenders—known in Britain as borstals and detention centers. While these offer their inmates a far busier life than most prisons, their attitude to offenders is imbued with the familiar refusal to allow them to be as responsible as they can be. Their treatment could not fail to be improved by practice in the facts of honest civilian life—that one works to pay for what one has and does.

Despite the benefits of the self-determinate sentence, it does raise some objections that would have to be dealt with before it became accepted. One of the strongest of these is that during periods of high unemployment, it would decrease the number of jobs available to civilians. This is a problem that needs to be viewed in perspective: In Britain, for example, there are about 40,000 prisoners and, even at this time of depression, some 24 million people in work; which means that if every working prisoner relinquished one hour's employment in order to increase the work available to civilians, this would add about ten seconds to the average working week outside. If the argument against prisoners working were taken to its logical conclusion so that they did no work at all, this would add less than seven minutes to the civilian working week. The benefit of that, compared with the benefits of prisoners working full-time and compensating their victims is so negligible that it would not appeal to most citizens as the better solution. The fundamental bases of good employment figures are sound political measures, not the idleness of prisoners.

There is also the objection that if prisoners worked under trade-union conditions, they would assume the power to strike. So they might, but in striking they would succeed in lengthening their time in custody so that it would be unlikely to be a popular practice.

An objection offenders might make to the self-determinate sentence would be the possibility of it encouraging their victims to overstate the damage or loss sustained in order to increase the compensation awarded. Such overstatement would, of course, be an offense in itself.

Another objection is that the self-determinate sentence would only provide compensation for victims of convicted offenders where victims of offenders not apprehended would still not receive restitution. This must necessarily remain the underlying principle of the self-determinate sentence, not only because its primary aim is to make offenders themselves responsible for paying reparation but also because courts could not cope administratively and national exchequers would be reluctant to cope financially with ordering and paying compensation for crimes for which no one had been found responsible.

The most powerful objection to the self-determinate sentence would come from the criminal underworld: from those who make their living organizing the receiving, threats, alibis, "protection" that are the requisites of a professional criminal's life. These people have no need at present to fear prison or police inquiries. Many are known to the police, who find it impossible to proceed against them. The self-determinate sentence would make evidence more readily available. The code of silence about confederates would be broken if silence entailed having to work in prison until the confederate's share of a crime was paid for as well as one's own. Any who shared in crime would go in fear of being named by an apprehended colleague. The security of the underworld would be disrupted. To prevent this, the opposition of the underworld to the self-determinate sentence would be fierce, organized, subtle, and backed by its wealth of money and influence. This is one of the best recommendations for the self-determinate sentence.

Anyone inclined to have sentimental objections about major offenders having to work for years to repair their crimes, might care to consider the following points:

1. The chances of a criminal going scot-free are at present better than sporting.

2. The self-determinate sentence offers the offender the opportunity of a reduced sentence if goods illegally obtained are voluntarily restored.

3. Major crimes are nonessential crimes. It is possible for people to steal a few pounds because of difficulty in making ends meet, or because, for psychological reasons, they need help: Prisons are staffed to provide the help needed by these offenders; the self-determinate sentence would demand of them only what their offense amounted to—a few pounds' worth of effort—while supplying the personal help needed. But major crimes are not crimes of need: They are acts of greed committed for gain by depriving other people. The only fair way to deal with them is to see that the gains are restored to those who have been deprived.

4. Those guilty of an offense who were found not responsible for their act would not be required to make compensation but would be treated in a mental hospital; and restitution by youths might be mitigated.

5. The remedy for any part of the self-determinate sentence to which an offender objected would be in his own hands: the simple expedient of avoiding crime.

To summarize the benefits of the self-determinate sentence, it would:

impose on prisoners work and responsibilities customary in civilian life; provide better justice for victims of crime; deter offenders by reducing crime from a paying proposition to one that has to be paid for; disrupt the solidarity of the underworld by adding to the mistrust of accomplices; increase the chances of offenders being apprehended because their confederates would be encouraged to name them; reduce the cost of maintaining prisoners; increase national productivity; render the work of the police and judiciary, prison staff and welfare workers more successful and satisfying; remove a large degree of injustice and degradation from the penal system; enable compensation to be ordered successfully in conjunction with all types of treatment for offenders, by ensuring that if an offender failed to make restitution as a civilian, he would be obliged to do so as a prisoner.

10 Restitution by Criminal Offenders: A Summary and Overview

Gilbert Geis

A criminal law exists; Someone is convicted of breaking that law. What is to be done to (or with) that person?

This is the question that has faced the participants in our Symposium. Their focus has been on one particular answer: that the offender be made to pay in some "meaningful" way for what he has done. It has been stressed that the payment by the law violator should either go directly to the crime victim or to the victim's heirs, or that it should take the form of community service, thereby contributing to the general social wellbeing.

Such restitution or reparation by the offender for his criminal behavior has been viewed as offering a number of advantages over present methods. For one thing, reparative payments to the victim could help to defray costs such as medical bills and wage losses that were incurred as a result of the victimization. For another, the process of restitution might create within the offender a sense of the true extent of the harm he had inflicted on another human being. Fiscal atonement could produce in the offender a feeling of having been cleansed, a kind of redemptive purging process, which might inhibit subsequent wrongdoing. The closer attachment of the penalty to the offense and the criminal to the victim have also been said to represent a method for bringing about justice superior to the present procedure in which the offender may pay a fine which goes to the State or may serve time in prison, where he will work for minimal or no wages or idle away his time.

The advantages of restitution seem so obvious that commentators find it barely believable at times that programs have not long since been set into motion. Note, for instance, the 1974 report of the Law Reform Commission of Canada:

Doesn't it seem to be a rejection of common sense that a convicted offender is rarely made to pay for the damage he has done? Isn't it surprising that the victim generally gets nothing for his loss? Restitution—making the offender pay or work to restore the damage—or, where this is not possible, compensation—payment from public funds to the victim for his loss—would seem to be a natural thing for sentencing policy and practice. Yet, under present law they are, more frequently than not, ignored.[1]

Nonetheless, as the Symposium papers make clear, the matter is far from simple. Indeed, the Canadian Law Reform Commission's views themselves were subject to some intensive and not overly friendly criticism by research workers at the University of Toronto's Centre of Criminology who noted, among many other things, that the fact that restitution has not been employed in Anglo-Saxon countries for so long, despite its seeming simplicity and logic, ought to give rise to some suspicion that the matter is not quite as uncomplicated as it appears to be at first glance.[2]

Certainly, a considerable portion of the appeal of restitution programs for dealing with criminal offenders lies in what is now generally regarded as the almost total bankruptcy of current correctional approaches. Imprisonment, in particular, has come to be seen as a counterproductive process, unable in general to deter subsequent criminal acts either in regard to the offender himself or those for whom he might serve as an object-lesson.[3] Treatment regimens for criminal offenders, most of them based on counseling modalities, have also come under severe attack, much of it founded on evaluations of their impact on criminal recidivism.[4]

In the fact of what is now regarded as correctional failure, the way lies open for inauguration of different approaches to dealing with criminal offenders. Besides restitution programs, ideas that have been put forward include the abolition of insanity pleas, swifter and surer sentencing, elimination of plea bargaining, reintroduction of capital punishment, decriminalization of so-called victimless crimes, diversion of offenders from incarceration into community treatment programs, and the abolition of the indeterminate sentence. Advocates of each of these positions see them as contributing to an alleviation of what is commonly regarded in the United States as an epidemic condition of criminal behavior.

Restitution may be seen, in this context, as one of a series of competing proposals for dealing with criminal activity, each maintaining that it will produce a more satisfactory result than present methods. The different proposed schemes are not necessarily contradictory or even mutually exclusive. It is possible that varying methods may be used to deal with different kinds of offenses and different kinds of offenders. At the same time it should be recognized that tampering with any aspect of the criminal justice system is apt to have considerable impact on other phases. A widespread restitution program will bear on police, court, and correctional procedures and bring about consequences that no degree of prescience can now discern.

What must be done, to carry the argument for restitution is to enunciate carefully and systematically the content and the rationale for such programs. Arguments can then be mounted that attempt to portray the consequences of the programs. In this regard, the stricture of the Swiss historian Jakob Burckhardt needs to be kept in the foreground when setting forth claims. "The worse form of tyranny," Burckhardt observed, "is the denial of complexity." Strenuous attempts will have to be made to measure accurately the alleged outcomes of restitutive approaches. At the same time it will have to be appreciated that such evaluations are as much or more personal and political tasks than social scientific ones. How, for example, does one compare a

2-percent decrease in the burglary rate with an extra expense of $4,000 for each case assigned to the restitution program? How are we to judge a restitution program that provides monetary aid for 5 percent of the jurisdiction's mugging victims but to achieve this result, imposes an average additional period of four month's State supervison on the muggers who committed the crimes for which restitution was ordered? No formulas exist that will allow scientific calculation of the verdict that should be reached on the basis of such facts. Indeed, the facts themselves convey but one very small part of the total story of what a restitution program might mean.

At any rate, intellectual humility would seem to be notably in order in regard to any alterations of correctional affairs, including the inauguration of restitution programs. A reading of the historical archives quickly produces sufficient material to cool off the most perfervid of reformers: Panegyrics abound in regard to correctional approaches which are now being harshly criticized as wicked and self-defeating. One early penal reformer noted, for instance, that "in the universal adoption of the indeterminate sentence with all that it logically involves, rests the strongest hope for final victory in the contest, which has heretofore been a losing contest, for the suppression of crime."[5] Similarly, the juvenile court, now criticized as undermining basic constitutional rights, was at its outset proclaimed in the following grandiloquent terms: "In this new court we tear down primitive prejudice, hatred, and hostility toward the lawbreaker in that most hide-bound of all human institutions, the court of law, and we will attempt, as far as possible to administer justice in the name of truth, love and understanding."[6] And who now would not snicker at the pious pronouncements of the progenitors of Pennsylvania's system of solitary confinement at labor for criminal offenders:

Shut out from a tumultuous world, and separated from those equally guilty with himself, he can indulge his remorse unseen, and find ample opportunity for reflection and reformation. His daily intercourse is with good men, who in administering to his necessities, animate his crushed hopes, and pour into his ear the oil of joy and consolation.[7]

The aim of the foregoing commentary is not to foment cynicism, but rather to put into perspective any zealous advocacy lacking elements of self-doubt. Restitution may indeed be a magnificent step forward in correctional arrangements, but it appears desirable to take that step, if it is to be taken at all, with a certain self-aware tentativeness.

The papers presented during the meetings at the First International Symposium on Restitution have varied in content, ranging over a considerable number of substantive and programmatic issues. It would be redundant, and would also be a disservice to the richness of the papers, to attempt to summarize in a rote manner what they say. Instead, the focus of this paper will be the three particular topics that seem to be of general importance. The matters that will be discussed are: (1) the historical record regarding restitution, including comments on the relationship between restitution and compensation to crime victims from public funds; (2) programmatic issues; and (3) concerns in evaluative studies of restitution.

Historical Issues

Some writers who favor the extension of restitution procedures to a much broader spectrum of correctional matters than they now cover adopt the rather romantic posture that restitution represents a criminal justice tradition of ancient times which was inopportunely abandoned. It is suggested that it is now more than proper to return to our fundamental, time-tested heritage.

It is true, of course, that historical experience ought not be ignored, but the halo that surrounds the history of restitution probably needs dismemberment. In a large measure, it appears, the movement of the state into the criminal justice arena, and its arrogation to itself of fines and confiscated goods, represented not primarily a matter of royal greed (though there was some of this too), but rather a reaction to popular distress at the awfulness of existing criminal justice arrangements.

Note, for instance, the ancient practice of "trial by ordeal," a matter which was, as Frederick Wines notes as "Nothing more or less than an appeal to the Almighty to perform a miracle in vindication of the innocence of the accused."[8] One form involved submersion of the bound body of a suspected offender into a lake. If the accused body sank and drowned, this was regarded as a sign that God was satisfied with the person's innocence since God was willing to bring the accused into divine domains. If the body floated, this was interpreted as divine rejection and a certain sign of guilt. The accused was, for this reason, promptly put to death. Disemboweling, macabre tortures and mutilations—these usages of medieval times ought to alert us that the criminal justice practices of our ancestors, of which restitution was a key element, were not apt to be notably benign.[9]

The practice of restitution was particularly suited for the wealthy since they readily could make amends for any infringement on the rights of others by drawing on their own funds, a matter which has contemporary relevance to consideration of guidelines for restitutive efforts. Or if they were strong enough, the guilty parties could merely ignore the plight of their victims. Only if they collectively came together behind the victim was there hope of reparation in such instances, and our ancestors were not that different from us: They backed the strong and ignored the weak. In point of fact, private programs of restitution, like much else in ancient times, served the purposes of the very powerful, and their elimination was one of the significant steps forward on the long and still largely untraveled path toward equal justice for all. Pollock and

Maitland, the leading scholars of the criminal law of olden times, note, for instance, that restitution as practiced during the twelfth century was a vicious enterprise. In particular, it served as a vehicle by means of which the lower classes could be pushed into slavery by those to whom they came to owe a restitutive obligation:

a *wīte* [fine] of 5 pounds was of frequent occurrence and to the ordinary tiller of the soil must have meant ruin. Indeed there is good reason to believe that for a long time past the system of *bōt* [indemnity] and *wīte* had been delusive, if not hypocritical. It outwardly reconciled the stern facts of a rough justice with a Christian reluctance to shed blood; it demanded money instead of life, but so much money that few were likely to pay it. Those who could not pay were outlawed or sold as slaves. From the very first it was an aristocratic system; not only did it make a distinction between those "dearly born" and those who were cheaply born, but it widened the gulf by impoverishing the poor folk. One unlucky blow resulting in the death of a thegn [noble] may have been enough to reduce a whole family of ceorls [serfs] to economic dependence or even to legal slavery. When we reckon up the causes which made the bulk of the nation into tillers of the lands of the lords, *bōt* and *wīte* should not be forgotten. . . .[10]

Contemporary revival of the idea of restitution as a keystone of penal policy is clearly traceable to the work of Margery Fry. In *Arms of the Law*, Ms. Fry proposed that offenders be made to pay victims to alleviate a portion of the harm they had inflicted. "Compensation cannot undo the wrong," Ms. Fry wrote, but

it will often assuage the injury, and it has real educative value for the offender, whether adult or child. Repayment is the best first step toward reformation that a dishonest person can make. It is often the ideal solution.[11]

The falling away of Ms. Fry from advocacy of restitution is worth note. By 1957 she had switched her support to a program of State compensation for crime victims, and she was citing the case of a court-restitution award of £11,500 to a man blinded in an assault. The amount was to be paid at the rate of 5 shilings a week, and would require 442 years for its total recovery. Behind Ms. Fry's endorsement of compensation to crime victims from public funds was the view that the State would have to assume the obligation of ameliorating deprivation suffered by its members as part of enlightened social policy. "The principle of clubbing together is venerable in British social life," Ms. Fry noted, and she drew a direct analogy to the industrial insurance program in concluding that "the logical way of providing for criminally inflicted injuries would be to tax every adult citizen . . . to cover a risk to which each is exposed."[12]

It is apparent that restitution schemes will have to be blended in some manner with the victim-compensation programs that now are appearing throughout the country.[13] Otherwise, the victims who will be helped by restitutive processes will represent an idiosyncratic and highly selective group. As LeRoy Schultz has observed, restitution as a condition of probation or parole is:

ineffectual in meeting the compensation needs of the great majority of victims because probationers and parolees are insolvent or, if employed, do not earn enough to exceed basic needs. In addition, not all offenders are apprehended; many may be juveniles; some will be incapable of responsibility due to mental illness; others may be acquitted due to technical or legal reasons; and many will not be granted probation or parole.[14]

Indeed, the pressure on criminals may be to run the risk of victimizing a dozen poor persons rather than one rich individual. If the offender is caught then and accused of a single offense (as is usually the case), the restitution to the poor person, in terms of the amount involved either as loot or as loss of wages by the victim would likely be less and therefore the restitutive conditions could be more readily met.

A particularly interesting aspect of restitution debates, one that has not emerged fully during the Symposium discussions, relates to its operation in regard to criminals who possess some wealth of their own. The annals of criminal law are replete with instances of well-to-do defendants who voluntarily offer restitution and thereby obtain mitigation of their sentence. Several states by law allow or have allowed for the "compromise" of misdemeanors through restitution; that is, the party aggrieved may appear in court and acknowledge that he has received satisfaction for his injury, whereupon the court may, in its discretion, discharge the defendant.[15]

Cases involving such statutes are instructive in pinpointing some of the issues that will undoubtedly arise in more far-reaching programs of restitution. In New York, for instance, before its repeal, three appeals arose from the misdemeanor compromise law.[16] In *People* v. *Bombace*[17] miscreants had damaged a New York City hotel room. The hotel owners estimated the cost to them at $245; during its hearing of the motion to dismiss, the court decided that a fairer price was $153. In another case[18] a woman had turned over half of her property to a man who had, she claimed, promised to marry her. When he failed to follow through on the alleged offer of marriage, she filed a suit demanding the property's return on the grounds of breach of promise. This plea failed since the court declared it to be contrary to public policy to have the property returned for such a reason. Then the man assaulted the woman, and on this occasion she "accepted" the return of her property as a compromise of the simple assault misdemeanor. On appeal, however, the court again ruled that the property should remain with the man. The judge argued that it was his role to determine the suitability of the terms of compromised cases; in this instance if the between-the-lines message is read correctly, the court seemed to have picked up the odor of a bit of blackmail.

The third appellate case under the New York statute[19] involved a man who failed to make contributions over a 15-month period to the Welfare and Pensions Fund as required by law. He subsequently paid up what he owed, and asked that the criminal case against him be closed. The court ruled against him, noting that compromises had to be negotiated with its participation. At best, the decision said, the restitution might be taken into account at the time of sentencing.

The California statute offers an appellate court decision[20] in which a person accused of hit-and-run driving attempted to repay the victim for his expenses and thereby to have the case dismissed. The appellate court ruled, however, that the offense did not involve a civil injury of the victim, but rather an offense against the public, and therefore it could not be compromised under the terms of the statute.

These cases offer the following lessons, among others: (1) that victims may inflate their claims against offenders, just as they do against insurance companies; and (2) that since restitution is likely to be regarded as a less-harsh-than-normal penalty, public and official resistance is apt to develop to its use when it is seen as defeating what is regarded as a fundamental sense of justice—or of vengeance.

Victims, prosecutors, judges, and juries are known to be lenient at times with offenders who offer to make what is regarded as appropriate restitution, particularly in the case of property losses. Indeed, the "perfect crime" is sometimes blueprinted as one in which an offender embezzles a large sum, spends it, and then about to be caught, embezzles a similarly large amount from the same victim. He then offers to return the second amount if he will not be prosecuted. It seems likely that few victims otherwise faced with the loss of the total sum, would not accede to this offer, at least if there were not bonding arrangements and if government authorities were not likely to be aroused. In fact, the victim might be especially moved to write the embezzler a highly laudatory letter of recommendation so that he could secure a responsible job with competitors.

Other issues raised by participants in the Symposium which deserve emphasis at this point include the following:

1. In terms of the historical record, there is a need to establish a contextual background that would indicate what conditions gave rise to restitutive schemes and what ends such schemes serve. In particular, cross-cultural studies of people who to this day employ restitution rather than incarceration should yield valuable insights into the dynamics and cultural roots of the process.

2. It was noted that the desire of states to support restitution programs may be a consequence of the fact that rather than gaining funds from criminal prosecutions, as in earlier times, these matters have become inordinately expensive. If financial aims solely undergird restitution advocacy, are these of sufficient persuasiveness to promote support of the programs? In particular, when the matter concerns—to use the words of one speaker—"trading dollars for liberty," there seems to be a particular need for careful and critical examination of proposals.

3. Satisfactory procedures for assessing damages subject to restitutive processes will have to be established. Many European countries use an "ad-

hesive" procedure[21] in which both civil and criminal liability is established as part of the same judicial hearing. All parties require careful protection of their rights if new restitutive approaches are to be inaugurated.

4. There will be a need to alter the traditional rules of prison labor and those applying to the sale of prison-manufactured goods, if inmates are to be expected to earn sums sufficient to allow them to pay for the damages they inflicted through criminal acts. One difficulty involves competition between free-world labor and prison labor. Particularly in periods of unemployment, the idea of training adjudicated criminals in skilled crafts and marketing their products—and particularly the idea of offering them employment when their restitutive obligation has been met—may smack a bit of overrewarding the "bad" at the expense of the "good."

A number of other items were also of particular interest during the discussions. One speaker, for instance, observed that restitution programs may appear promising because they "haven't yet clearly failed," though the same participant put aside this mild cynicism for a moment to say that, despite the "litany of problems" that he saw associated with restitution, he was "genuinely optimistic" about it, largely because he saw possibilities for greater fairness than currently prevails in the administration of criminal justice. Another speaker was skeptical (though not critical) about restitution because she found both the left and the right wing of the political spectrum supporting the matter. So widely endorsed a proposal might merely be bland and inoffensive, she thought, or perhaps it appealed to all but those unrepresented in the discussions, though most deeply involved in the proposals: the offenders.

The issue of "class" justice arose in the form of the question of whether restitutive sums ought to be pegged to the damage done or to the wherewithal of the offender. Someone wanted to know whether the white-collar worker would be allowed to sit behind a desk to earn the sum required by his restitutive contract, while the unskilled labor would do harder tasks and whether this was fair. Another person suspected that restitution would be assessed in instances in which the offender might more reasonably have been allowed to have another chance without any penalty except perhaps a period of supervision within the community. This "overpunishment" could induce bitterness and feelings of injustice in the offender.

The foregoing matters of discrimination among offenders and too-ready recourse to restitution (in lieu of milder responses) are both illustrated in a newspaper article which is characteristic of a considerable number of similar items that have been appearing in the nation's press. Indeed, the publicity that a judge will receive from imposing a restitution sentence today must be regarded as one of the particular attractions of such sentences.

In 1975 newspapers reported a disposition made in Miami, Florida, in which a defendant, in lieu of a five-year prison sentence, was ordered to pay $1,500 annually for five years to provide higher education for the victim's children. The offender had run a red light resulting in the death of the victim. The 35-year-old offender was also the father of two children and earned approximately $11,500 per year.

A telephone call I made to the defense attorney in the preceding case elicited the information that the disposition was initiated by the judge. A year after the sentence, all parties are said to be relatively pleased with the way the case was handled. But a question still must exist as to whether it is desirable to have a father of two small children pay $150 a month out of a salary of $11,500 to educate the offspring of a man killed when the offender ran a red light.

Many of the foregoing matters were well summarized in a review of the place of restitution in the criminal law which was written more than 35 years ago:

A thoughtful consideration of the place of restitution in the criminal law calls for more than speculation about the elusive boundary between "criminal" and "civil" wrongs or deduction from traditional concepts concerning the "state's interest" in crimes. What is required is an evaluation in terms of the deterrent and reformative potentialities of the requirement of restitution; the extent to which these potentialities are enhanced or diminished when restitution is exacted by private parties; and the comparative social values inherent in permitting individuals to compromise crimes, insisting that they be settled only under official supervision, or forbidding their settlement. Needless to say, there may be room for different results depending upon the nature of the crime, the character of the offender, and other relevant factors. . . . [22]

Programmatic Issues

The last three lines of the preceding quotation set the stage for discussion of programmatic issues in restitution. The combinations and permutations of potential program approaches render the issues rather complex. Speakers at the Symposium described quite different blueprints that were used in Iowa, Georgia, Minnesota, and England. But none could offer more than barebone and noncomparable assessments of the possible impacts of these different kinds of arrangements.

The matter of program form might best be reduced to a common theme by examining categories of issues associated with various components of the efforts. A ready formula for such analysis lies in the common journalistic question: Who does what to whom with what intent and with what results?

Who?

Administration of restitution programs can be located at virtually any point along the criminal justice continuum. Police, courts, probation and/or parole offices, and prisons may serve to operate or to coordinate a restitution endeavor.

The comparative advantage of one or another arrangement is at best a matter of speculation.

A restitution effort might also be separated from traditional criminal justice auspices and administered by an existing or a newly established public or private agency. Certainly, the punitive connotation associated with currently operating criminal justice organizations probably puts them at some disadvantage in attempting to transmit a sense of concern for equity and for the welfare of both offender and victim. Social service agencies also might be better equipped, at least for dealing with the requirements of victims, if not those of offenders. A study by Sylvia Fogelman, for instance, of 49 persons who had collected victim-compensation money in California found them to constitute "a truly needy population left on its own to secure help, left unattended and rejected by the very government which it had looked to for protection and consideration."[23] The subjects reported a host of emotional and social needs attendant on their victimization. Thirty-five of the 49 respondents indicated that they wanted "just someone to talk to," or someone "to help them sort out their problems and help them get back on their feet" following their victimization. Eleven of the group reported losing friends because of the crime. Thirty of the 49 indicated that they had suffered some form of permanent physical injury as a result of the victimization. In short, and importantly, these victims sought not only restitution but also kindness and emotional sustenance. It seems arguable that they will be apt to obtain these things very effectively in a program of restitution operated under the auspices of criminal justice agencies.

Does What?

This matter forms the core of the restitutive approach. Various kinds of proposals for the nature of the effort that would make up the restitution program were put forward during the Symposium. In England, it was noted, restitutive efforts take the form of convicted persons performing public services which stand to benefit the community. In particular, they help persons such as the elderly and the handicapped, thereby not only providing aid but also deriving a sense of self-satisfaction. Note, for example, the response to one offender assigned to assisting elderly and disabled persons by providing bus trips and shopping expeditions:

I have been asked by the passengers of the community bus to write to you on their behalf to thank you for Colin and the wonderful work he is doing. He is not only an artist at driving. He has that reassuring personality so essential when taking invalids who have not ventured out of their homes for some time. His skill and indefinable something has made these people ask to be included in trip after trip. Many passengers expressed their affection for him in tangible ways by inviting him and his family to tea, etc.

Despite such glowing endorsement, it remains arguable whether many or few of the offenders who might be assigned to such duties would do them gracefully or efficiently, or whether they would perform in sullen and deceitful ways, regarding the chores as vengeful impositions or stupidly indulgent kinds of leniency.

One of the speakers, a pioneer writer in the field of restitution, maintained that "creative restitution," as he labeled his plan, would forcefully tend to induce a sense of almost religious catharsis in the offender. Under his scheme, the offender would be able to volunteer to make amends for his behavior. The offender's "active, effortful" behavior, it was argued, would replace the passive, destructive kinds of sentences that now follow criminal conviction. Perhaps so—perhaps not. Child-support orders in the marital arena provides an intriguing analog. Such support may reasonably be regarded as the decent contribution of (most always) the father to the nurture of his children. But many divorced men do not grant the reasonableness of the fiscal obligation that courts impose on them. They often perceive such payments as a matter of unjust enrichment on the part of their former mates or as an unconscionable burden on their own existence. Given this considerable resistance to paying out money for the support of one's own children, it appears likely that a sizeable number of persons caught up in restitutive schemes are going to harbor feelings of some anger about the monies they contribute from the fruits of the labor they perform.

For one of the proposed restitutive schemes, the blueprint involves "constructive" prison labor at market-value wages, with the prison experience parenthetically conveying proper work attitudes and the self-discipline necessary to succeed in the outside world. Other approaches put forward are more conventional. In Iowa the program involves regular work of the sort the offender was (or at least should have been) accustomed to, with a percentage of the wages going to the victim. Here, as elsewhere, the program is particularly careful to see that not so much is subtracted from the individual's income as to render his work without meaning except as it inoculates him against a worst fate such as incarceration.

One aspect of the Minnesota program uniquely attempts to bring the offender and the victim together to work out the details of the restitutive program. The reestablishment of the dyad situation which constituted the form of the original criminal event has a moral and esthetic appeal, though it is highly debatable whether the consequences for the parties are meretricious or commendable; or, put another way, it is not yet known what happens to what persons and under what circumstances when this arrangement is used.

Little discussion centered on other approaches such as those that tend to be reported in the mass media, involving rather "cute" responses to criminal events. These are apt to take the biblical form of an "eye for an eye," that is, to duplicate in some seemingly approximate fashion the original criminal event. Thus the vandals who put the classroom into disarray will be sentenced to reestablish it in its original condition. The drunk driver will be required to serve a certain number of days with the emergency ambulance crew that fetches back to the hospital the bodies of victims of driving mishaps. Again it remains arguable whether these "symbolic" forms of restitution are effective in inducing the kinds of attitudes and behaviors they aspire to bring about. Perhaps all that needs to be said for them, though, is that some of them tend to restore conditions to their earlier, precrime form, a result which at least provides some surcease for the unfortunate victim of the depradation.

To Whom?

Defining eligibility for participation in restitution programs constitutes one of the less troublesome program issues since the nature of the participating population will be determined largely by the character of the program itself—its ethos, its aims, and its approach. If the program is to operate inside a secure prison unit, then there will be no need to screen out offenders. If it is to involve community work under loose or no supervision, then public concerns might dictate that individuals who represent threats of violence or who have records for fleeing a jurisdiction be excluded from the program.

Eligibility might also be governed in terms of the kinds of offenses deemed suitable for reparation response. This area is something of a quagmire. How, for instance, are personal offenses to be denominated in monetary terms? Is rape worth $5,000 or $10,000 to the victim?—or are we to concentrate only on actual out-of-pocket expenses such as wage losses and medical bills rather than such amorphous items as pain and suffering? If so, is it fair that a student or a housewife cannot collect for loss of wages, though they are unable to resume their work for extended periods of time?

How about the matter of voluntary participation in restitutive efforts? May an offender opt to serve a suitable period of time in prison, taking his ease if he chooses, rather than participate in a restitutive scheme on the outside? How about Kathleen Smith's idea of a "self-determinate" sentence, under which an offender who does not pay his crime-induced debt will not be released from incarceration until/unless he does so with wages realized from productive labor? The "self-determinate" idea has little appeal for me, though Ms. Smith presented and defended it with considerable elan. One can envision a viciously rebellious institution population, defining itself (with some justice) as being further victimized by a class system that already had imposed considerable barriers against its achievement of a reasonable standard of living. And I see (in terms of how I imagine I would act) some likelihood of permanent harm being inflicted on victims by offenders desperate to avoid being apprehended and thrust into a "self-determinate" program. In Ms. Smith's system her penal institution "would be the immediate home for major or persistent offenders and the ultimate destination for other offenders who were permitted, but failed, to pay restitution in noncustodial surroundings." This idea comes close to imprisonment for debt, a matter deemed unconstitutional in the United States. Note, for instance, the decision of the California Supreme Court in *In re Trombley:*

Although by its terms the constitutional prohibition is directed to imprisonment in civil actions, it has been held to apply in a criminal proceeding where it appears that the legislation under which the accused is charged constitutes an attempt to make the mere act of failing to pay a debt a crime. The courts will not permit the purposes of the constitutional provision forbidding imprisonment for debt to be circumvented by mere form. . . .[24]

With What Intent?

Presumably, the ideal restitution program is one in which the offender repays the victim for the damage that has been caused. Fundamental questions need to be answered, however, such as whether the program seeks to aid the victim or the offender, when the interests of the two parties come in conflict, as they often will. For the offender a major aim is to indoctrinate him with a work discipline and to transmit a sense of satisfaction with legal labor that persists beyond the point that his criminally incurred debt has been paid off. For the victim hopefully there will be a dissipation of the sense of fury and anguish that often accompanies his state.[25] He will gain confidence in the operation of the criminal justice system, develop some greater tolerance for the offender, and himself continue to function in what is defined as a satisfactory manner. The state could benefit by having to expend less money on penal arrangements and on victim rehabilitation (e.g., welfare costs). Ideally, too, the general public will come to apprehend that restitution programs promote justice in a more decent way than had been accomplished under previously existing programs.

Each of these conditions, and many others, require painstaking scrutiny when seeking to determine the accomplishments of restitutive programs. Too often evaluations concentrate almost exclusively on recidivism statistics, in which calculations are made of the number of arrests and convictions and technical violations of the persons involved in the program. Beyond the evaluative astigmatism of such a focus, I would argue that traditional recidivism measures often are quite misleading. For one thing, recidivism represents the end product of an elaborate process that often does not bear any particularly exact relationship to the behavior involved. That is, there are apt to be considerably more criminal acts committed than there are to be apprehensions for such acts; and it is the acts that should interest us, not the varying competence and luck of the law-enforcement agencies. Technical violations too often are closely related to the nature of an intervention program rather than to the character of the individual participant's behavior. I would argue that determination of the outcome of a restitution program ought to attempt to secure scrupulous reports from the participants about what they have done and ought not to rely on official data regarding what has been observed and acted against. And such measures must be fleshed out very thoroughly with a variety of indexes of participant and public satisfaction with the operation of the program. In this way, it becomes possible for a policy maker to have at hand information addressing the efficacy of the program in meeting an entire spectrum of goals rather than only one or a very few truncated ones.

With What Results?

Many of the foregoing observations pertain to ascertainment of the outcome of the intervention as well as to its general aims. In addition, it seems desirable that very far-ranging inquiries be directed toward determination of the impact of the program upon eddying matters that might not at first glance appear to be related to it. It is possible, for instance, that a comprehensive restitution program might undercut general deterrence because it appears to represent wondrous leniency and therefore less threat to persons contemplating criminal activity. If so, then crime rates might rise in general while perhaps declining in the target population. It is very difficult, of course, to maintain that the intervention itself might have produced the general crime rise (except perhaps if the increase is found only in jurisdictions with restitution efforts and not at all in those without programs, and if there are a large number of both types scattered about). It is also worth determining whether a particular program merely serves to relocate criminal activity, just as higher penalties for prostitution in, say, New York City, may merely induce the prostitutes to migrate to Newark or Philadelphia.

It might also be noted—since this matter arose in one of the Symposium discussions—that the fairest measure of criminal activity associated with a restitution program is that which concentrates on public danger and not on a crime/time exposure ratio. That is, if a randomly selected control group is kept in prison for 8 months longer than an experimental group which is involved in a free-world restitution program and if the focus is on criminal activity, then the experimental group ought to be obligated to produce less crime during a specified period (say, 24 months) than the control group produced during the 16 months its members were on the streets. Too many researchers compare the periods of freedom for both groups. From the public's viewpoint, being mugged by an offender in a restitution program who might otherwise have been incarcerated seems, to me, to constitute a clear-cut failure that ought not be covered up by artificially regularizing the period of measurement.

A summary of the arrangements under which restitution might be conducted comes back to the fact that, given that we know very little about the value of any particular approach in contrast to another, the matter of the optimal and proper approach to restitution must be seen as an open question. Certainly, considerations such as efficiency, utility, humaneness among very many others, can dictate preference for one approach rather than another. But as far as accurate appraisals of the actual consequences of differing regiments go, we simply do not now have sufficient information to allow for an informed judgment.

Evaluation Issues

It is a cliché of intervention strategies that any proposed program requires careful, almost exquisite, evaluation if we are to learn truly about its consequences. Two themes might be stressed here: The first concerns experimental design and the second relates to the necessity for a considerable amount of descriptive material about restitution programs that are undergoing evaluation.

I do not go along with the common view that an experimental correctional program ought to introduce as little perturbation as possible into the system; that is, that everything ought to be kept exactly as before except for the element that is being evaluated. Given the bleak history of experimental endeavors in corrections, I much prefer that a new program be mounted with every conceivable asset that it can command. It ought to have the best workers, rich financing, low case loads, and any other kinds of assistance it can manage. If it then is proven to be a "success," at least it can be said that there is some amalgam that works. What the bare essentials of that successful endeavor are is what might next be determined.

The reason for my preference for this approach is that no matter how "clean" the experimental design, there really is no way of knowing with any precision whether it was the barebones intervention ethos or some other aspect of the new program that produced the measured outcome. Researchers who say they have, for instance, evaluated the halfway-house concept in corrections when they have, in truth, only enumerated the outcome of one particular halfway-house endeavor are, to my mind, generalizing much too far beyond their data. The setting of the halfway house, the economic conditions in the society at the time, idiosyncratic events in the facility, and a host of other circumstances— these all contribute in largely unknown and unknowable ways to the outcome of an intervention program, and it is quite impossible to take the results far beyond the particular situation, except in the most tentative manner. As Edward Suchman noted: "Program testing has almost no generalizability, being applicable solely to the specific programs being evaluated.[26]

It is for this reason that I believe that interventions such as restitution efforts require an inordinate amount of descriptive information to accompany any statistical measures. I have elaborated on this theme elsewhere.[27] Perhaps it is only worth noting further that the need to monitor interventions such as restitution programs is of fundamental importance. Some years ago the British command paper known as the *Seerbohm Report* well stated the essential need for such evaluation work: "It is both wasteful and irresponsible to set experiments in motion and omit to record and analyze what happens." The report also noted, "It makes no sense in terms of administrative efficiency, and, however little intended, it indicates a careless attitude toward human welfare."[28]

Conclusion

Restitution, it seems to me, is clearly an idea that merits a serious test in terms of its ability to alleviate some of the severe problems besetting efforts to deal with crime and criminals in the United States today. It may bring about better feelings in citizens about the quality of justice in their country; it may prove of value to victims; and it may help criminals to appreciate the nature of the harm they inflict on others. It may also serve to alleviate offender's alienation from a law-abiding existence. The conferees throughout the Symposium took pains to stress that they did not view restitution as a panacea but rather saw it as a possible meliorative approach. They did not want to oversell the idea and then have to deal with unfulfilled aspirations. Instead, they preferred to promise little, but to hope for much more—and to see what happens.

It is interesting that Minnesota, the site of the First International Symposium on Restitution, is the only state in the United States—and, indeed, the only jurisdiction in the Anglo-Saxon legal world—where in a criminal trial, the defense has the last word to the jury.[29] It seems appropriate, then, to conclude my observations on the preliminary hearing that restitution has undergone in Minnesota these last two days with a positive note in defense of the concept. That note would suggest that restitution appears to offer some hope that an element of empathy might be introduced into criminal justice business. It seems to me that the failure of the offender to identify his interests with those of the victim represents the worst horror of predatory criminal activity, and its worst threat to a decent way of life. In China, urban law-breakers sometimes are sentenced to do time in the countryside so that they may absorb the spirit and the ethos of persons who are regarded as heroic by the State. This procedure related to the perceived need of a healthy society to close the distance between its peoples; to create feelings of relationship and common purpose so that one group does not consider itself free to exploit another. It is undoubtedly easier to attempt to force empathy through the use of authoritarian tactics. Restitution may represent in a democratic state a step toward the same end, that of creating sympathetic bonds among people. It certainly deserves a chance to demonstrate if, in fact, it can fulfill this crucial purpose.

Notes

1. Canadian Law Reform Commission, *Restitution and Compensation-Fines* (Ottawa: Information Canada, 1974), p. 5.

2. Philip Stenning and Sergio Ciano, "Restitution and Compensation and Fines," *Ottawa Law Review* (Spring 1975): 316-329.

3. American Friends Service Committee, *Struggle for Justice: A Report on Crime and Punishment in America* (New York: Hill and Wang, 1971).

4. Robert Martinson, "What works?: Questions and Answers About Prison Reform," *Public Interest* 35 (1974): 22-54.

5. Eugene Smith, "Indeterminate Sentence For Crime," *Independent* 58 (May 11, 1905): 1052-1056.

6. H.H. Lou, *Juvenile Courts in the United States* (Chapel Hill: University of North Carolina Press, 1927), p. 2.

7. Harry E. Barnes and Negley K. Teeters, *New Horizons in Criminology* (New Jersey: Prentice-Hall, 1943), p. 513.

8. Frederick H. Wines, *Punishment and Reformation* (New York: Crowell, 1923), pp. 45-46.

9. George R. Scott, *The History of Corporal Punishment* (London: Torchstream, 1938).

10. Frederick Pollock and Frederic W. Mapland, *The History of English Law Before the Time of Edward I*, 2d ed. (Cambridge: Cambridge University Press, 1968), Vol. 2, pp. 460-462.

11. Margery Fry, *Arms of the Law* (London: Victor Gollancz, 1951), p. 16.

12. Margery Fry, "Justice for Victims," *Journal of Public Law* 8 (Spring 1959): 191-194.

13. Herbert Edelhertz and Gilbert Geis, *Public Compensation to Victims of Crime* (New York: Praeger, 1974).

14. LeRoy G. Schultz, "The Violated: A Proposal to Compensate Victims of Violent Crime," *Saint Louis University Law Journal* 10 (Winter 1965): 243.

15. Richard E. Laster, "Criminal Restitution: A Survey of Its Past History and an Analysis of Its Present Usefulness," *University of Richmond Law Review*, 5 (Fall 1970): 87.

16. New York Code Crim., Proc. 88663-666.

17. *People v. Bombace* (1957), 17 Misc2d 9, 184 NYS2d 753.

18. *Hallstrom v. Erkas* (1953), 124 NYS 2d 169.

19. *People v. Trapp* (1965), 260 NYS2d 305.

20. *People v. O'Rear* (1963), 34 CalRptr 1961, 220 CA2dSupp 927.

21. Stephen Schafer, *Restitution to Victims of Crime* (London: Stevens, 1960).

22. "Restitution and Criminal Law," *Columbia Law Review* 39 (November 1939): 1185-1207.

23. Sylvia Fogelman, "Compensation to Victims of Crime of Violence—The Forgotten Program," M.S.W. thesis (Los Angeles: University of Southern California, 1971), p. 47.

24. In *re Trombley* (1948), 31 Cal2d 801, 193 P2d 734.

25. Gilbert Geis, "Victims of Crimes of Violence and the Criminal Justice System," in *Violence and Criminal Justice*, eds. Duncan Chappell and John Monahan (Lexington, Mass.: Lexington Books, 1975), p. 6174.

26. Edward A. Suchman, *Evaluative Research* (New York: Russell Sage Foundation, 1967), p. 77.

27. Gilbert Geis, "Program Descriptions in Criminal Justice Research," in *Criminal Justice Research*, ed. Emilio Viano (Lexington, Mass.: Lexington Books, 1975), pp. 87-95.

28. *Report of the Committee on Local Authority and Allied Personal Social Services*, Command Paper 3703 (London: Her Majesty's Stationery Office, 1968).

29. Marilyn Kunkel and Gilbert Geis, "Order of Final Argument in Minnesota Criminal Trials," *Minnesota Law Review* 42 (March 1958): 549-558.

Appendixes

Appendix A:
Survey of Nineteen
Operational Restitution
Programs

Restitution programs included in the July 1976 Survey of 19 Operational Restitution Programs

Alberta

Pilot Alberta Restitution Center
534 Eighth Avenue S.W.
Calgary, Alberta   T2P1E8

Arizona

Pima County Attorney's Adult Diversion Project
Pima County Attorney's Office
131 West Congress Street—Suite 600
Tucson, Arizona   85701

Georgia

Albany Restitution Center
Box 691, 418 Society Avenue
Albany, Georgia   31701

Atlanta Restitution Center
39 Eleventh Street N.E.
Atlanta, Georgia   30309

Macon Restitution Center
873 Cherry Street
Macon, Georgia   31208

Rome Restitution Center
Northwestern Regional Hospital
Redmond Road
Rome, Georgia   30161

Iowa

Restitution in Probation Experiment
Department of Court Services
1000 College Avenue
Des Moines, Iowa   50314

Maryland

Community Arbitration Program
102 Cathedral Street
Annapolis, Maryland   21401

Minnesota

Minnesota Restitution Center
930 South Fifth Street
Minneapolis, Monnesota   55400

Nevada

Victims' Assistance Program
County Juvenile Court
Las Vegas, Nevada

New York

Arbitration as an Alternative to the Criminal Warrant
(American Arbitration Association)
Community Dispute Services
140 West 51 Street
New York, New York   10020

Ohio

Night Prosecutor's Program
120 West Gay Street
Columbus, Ohio   43215

Ontario

Rideau-Carlton Restitution Project
900 Lady Ellen Place
Ottawa, Ontario   K1Z5L5

Victim-Offender Reconciliation Project
Eight Water Street North
Kitchener, Ontario   N2H5A5

Oregon

Washington County Restitution Center
Department of Public Safety
146 N.E. Lincoln Street
Hillsboro, Oregon   97123

South Dakota

Seventh Circuit Court Victim's Assistance Program
Pennington County Courthouse
Rapid City, South Dakota   57701

Utah

Restitution Work Program
Youth Inc.
Salt Lake City, Utah

Washington

Community Accountability Program
Youth Services Bureau
Seattle, Washington

Wisconsin

Restitution and Effective Diversion from the
   Criminal Justice System
Financial and Debt Counseling Service Inc.
2218 North Third Street
Milwaukee, Wisconsin 53212

Appendix B:
LEAA-funded Adult
Restitution Programs, 1976

Restitution Project
California Department of
  Corrections
714 P Street
Sacramento, California 95814

Colorado Crime Victims Restitution
  Program
Office of the Governor
136 State Capitol Building
Denver, Colorado 80203

Restitution Service
Connecticut Judicial Department
P.O. Box 1350
231 Capitol Avenue
Hartford, Connecticut 06101

Sole Sanction Restitution Program
Department of Corrections/Offender
  Rehabilitation
800 Peachtree Street, Room 321
Atlanta, Georgia 30308

Maine Restitution Project
Department of Mental Health and
  Corrections/Maine State Bar Association
State Office Building, Room 411
Augusta, Maine 04330

Massachusetts Parole Board
100 Cambridge Street
Boston, Massachusetts 02202

Project Repay
Office of the District Attorney, Room 600
Multnomah County Courthouse
Portland, Oregon 97204

Selected References

Bentham, Jeremy. *The Works of Jeremy Bentham.* Edinburgh: William Tait, 1838, Part 2, pp. 371-375, 386-388.

Bergman, Howard S. "Community Service In England: An Alternative to Custodial Sentence." *Federal Probation,* March 1975, pp. 43-46.

Bersheid, Ellen, and Walster, Elaine. "When Does a Harm-Doer Compensate a Victim?" *Journal of Personality and Social Psychology* 6 (1967): 435-441.

Bersheid, Ellen; Walster, Elaine; and Barclay, A. "The Effect of Time on the Tendency to Compensate a Victim." *Psychological Reports* 25 (1969): pp. 431-436.

Canadian Journal of Corrections. "Compensation to Victims of Crime and Restitution by Offenders." 10 (1968): 591-599.

Carlsmith, J. Merrill, and Gross, Alane. "Some Effects of Guilt on Compliance." *Journal of Personality and Social Psychology* 11 (1969): pp. 232-239.

Cohen, Irving E. "The Integration of Restitution in the Probation Services." *Journal of Criminal Law, Criminology and Police Science* 34 (1944): 351-321.

Del Vecchio, Giorgio. "The Problem of Penal Justice." *Revista Jurdica De La Universidad de Purto Rico* 27 (1957-1958): 65-81.

Dockar-Drysdale, B. "Damage and Restitution." *British Journal of Delinquency,* July 1953, pp. 4-13.

Edelhertz, Herbert. *Restitutive Justice: A General Survey and Analysis.* Law and Justice Study Center, Battelle Human Affairs Research Centers, Seattle, Washington, January 1975.

Eglash, Albert. "Creative Restitution." *Journal of Criminal Law,* March-April 1958, pp. 619-622.

_____. "Creative Restitution: Some Suggestions for Prison Rehabilitation Programs." *American Journal of Corrections,* November-December 1958, pp. 20-34.

_____. "Creative Restitution: Its Roots in Psychiatry, Religion, & Law." *British Journal of Delinquency,* May 10, 1960, pp. 182-190.

_____, and Holzchuk, Karl. "Creative Restitution in the Treatment of Offenders In Germany." *Journal of Social Therapy* 4 (1960): pp. 213-216.

Fogel, David; Galaway, Burt; and Hudson, Joe, "Restitution in Criminal Justice: A Minnesota Experiment." *Criminal Law Bulletin* 8 (1972): pp. 681-691.

Freedman, Jonathan L.; Wallington, Sue Ann; and Bless, Evelyn. "Compliance Without Pressure: The Effect of Guilt." *Journal of Personality and Social Psychology* 7 (1967): pp. 117-124.

Fry, Margery. *Arms of the Law*. London: Victor Gollancz, 1951.

_____. "Justice for Victims." *Journal of Public Law* 8 (1959): pp. 191-194.

Galaway, Burt, and Hudson, Joe. "Restitution and Rehabilitation." *Crime and Delinquency* 18 (1972): 403-410.

_____, and Hudson, Joe. "Issues in the Correctional Implementation of Restitution to Victims of Crime." *Considering the Victim: Selected Readings in Restitution and Victim Compensation*, eds. Joe Hudson and Burt Galaway. Springfield, Illinois: Thomas Press, 1975.

Garofalo, Raffaele. *Criminology*. Boston: Little, Brown and Company, 1914, pp. 419-435.

Harding, John K. "Community Service—A Beginning." *Probation* (England) 19 (1973): 13-17.

Heinz, Joe; Galaway, Burt; and Hudson, Joe, "Restitution or Parole: A Follow-up Study of Adult Offenders. *Social Service Review* 50 (1976): pp. 148-156.

Hobhouse, L.T. *Morals in Evolution*. London: Chapman and Hall, 1951.

Hudson, Joe, and Galaway, Burt. *Considering the Victim: Selected Readings in Restitution and Victim Compensation*. Springfield, Illinois: Thomas Press, 1975.

Hudson, Joe, and Galaway, Burt. "Crime Victims and Public Social Policy." *Journal of Sociology and Social Welfare* III (1976): pp. 629-635.

_____, and Galaway, Burt. "Undoing the Wrong." *Social Work* 19: May 1974.

Jacob, Bruce R. "Reparation or Restitution by the Criminal Offender to His Victim: Applicability of an Ancient Concept in the Modern Correctional Process." *Journal of Criminal Law, Criminology and Police Science* 61 (1970): 152-167.

Jacobson, William T. "Use of Restitution in the Criminal Process: People Versus Miller." *U.C.L.A. Law Review* 16 (1969): 456-475.

Kaufman, Clementine L. "Community Service Volunteers: A British Approach to Delinquency Prevention." *Federal Probation* 37 (1973): pp. 35-41.

Keve, Paul, and Eglash, Albert. "Payments On A Debt to Society." *NPPA News* 36 (1957): pp. 1-2.

Kole, Janet. "Arbitration as an Alternative to the Criminal Warrant." *Judicature* 56 (1973): pp. 295-297.

Lamborn, Leroy L. "Toward a Victim Orientation in Criminal Theory." *Rutgers Law Review* 22 (1968): 733-768.

Laster, Richard E. "Criminal Restitution: A Survey of its Past History and an Analysis of its Present Usefulness." *University of Richmond Law Review* 5 (1970): pp. 80-98.

Macauley, Stewart, and Walster, Elaine. "Legal Structures and Restoring Equity." *Journal of Social Issues* 27 (1971): 173-188.

MacNamara, Donal E.J., and Sullivan, John. "Composition, Restitution, Compensation: Making the Victim Whole." *Urban Review* 6 (1973): pp. 23-31.

More, Thomas. *Utopia.* London. J.C. Collins edition, 1904, pp. 23-24.

Mowrer, O.H. "Loss and Recovery of Community" in George M. Gazda, ed., *Innovations to Group Psychotherapy.* Springfield, Illinois: Thomas Press, 1968.

Overland, Mark E., and Newhouse, James. "Juvenile Criminal Law in the Federal Republic of Germany and in England." *California Western Law Review* 4 (1968): 35-64.

Palmer, John W. "Pre-Arrest Diversion: Victim Confrontation." *Federal Probation* 38 (1974): pp. 12-18.

Pease, K.; Durkin, P.; Earnshaw, I.; Payne, D.; and Thorpe, J. *Community Service Orders.* London: Her Majesty's Stationery Office, 1975.

Schafer, Stephen. "The Proper Role of a Victim-Compensation System." *Crime and Delinquency* 21 (1975): 45-49.

_____. *Compensation and Restitution to Victims of Crime.* Montclair, N.J.: Patterson Smith, 1970.

Smith, Kathleen. *A Cure for Crime: The Case for the Self-Determinate Prison Sentence.* London: Duckworth, 1965.

Spencer, Herbert. *Essays: Scientific Political & Speculative*, Vol. III. New York: D. Appleton & Company, 1892, pp. 152-191.

Index

Adhesive procedure, in legal systems, 48
Assessment of damages, 72, 153-154

Blood feud, 45
Blumberg, Abraham, 19, 20, 21

Civil court, effectiveness, 47-48, 56
Civil restitution, 40-41, 72
Clan system, and restitution, 36
Class, social. *See* Social class
Collective liability, restitution in societies with, 28-30, 33-34, 35-36, 41
Community, role in community service, 107-109, 115-117
Community service, case illustrations, 121-127; community acceptance, 107-109; and courts, 109-111; effectiveness, 116-117; evaluation, 117-119; future growth, 119-120; implementation, 107-112; implications, 120; legislation, 101-102; long-term, 120; offender view of, 41-42, 55, 98, 156-157; organization, 102-105; and prison population, 117; purpose, 105-107; role of community, 115-117; role of probation officer, 111-112; selection of offenders for, 112-113; tasks, 113-115, 129-130; types of, 105, 106, 109, 110. *See also* Compensation; Restitution; Restitution program; Victim compensation program
Compensation, and courts, 135-136; definition, 27-28; legislation, 52-53; method, 138; and parole, 139; payment to state, 46-47; in property versus violent crime, 135; in small-scale society, 46; state, 52-53; versus restitution, 23-24, 51, 64, 151-152. *See also* Community service; Restitution

Compensation program, and restitution program, 23-24; state, 48-49, 56, 58, 151-152. *See also* Restitution program; Victim compensation program
Composition. *See* Compensation
Correctional measures, alternate, 148
Correctional program, experimental, 161. *See also* Criminal justice system; Compensation program; Restitution program; Victim compensation program
Courts, assessment role, 134, 135, 136; civil, 47-48, 56; and community service, 109-111; and compensation, 135-136; small claims, 41
Creative restitution, 91-92, 93-96
Crime, corporate versus individual, 42; property versus violent, 56, 69-70, 135, 137-138; relation to sentence, 144; and restitution, 152. *See also* Murder; Recidivism
Crime rate, growth, 23; and restitution program, 131, 160
Criminal justice system, adhesive procedure, 48; comparison of, 47-48; and equality, 42; historical changes in, 47; neglect of victim, 19, 20-21, 22, 24, 40; and offender, 19-20, 40; reforms, 148; and restitution, 13-14, 47-49, 53-54, 64-66, 83, 87, 96; shift from family to state control, 47; support of, 22-23. *See also* Courts; Legislation; Police department; Probation officer
Criminal underworld, and self-determinate sentence, 145

Damages, actual versus common-law, 69; assessment of, 72, 153-154; psychological, 134; victim, median, 68-70. *See also* Liability

177

List of Contributors

Elaine Combs-Schilling
Department of Anthropology
University of California
Berkeley, California

Herbert Edelhertz
Senior Research Scientist
Battelle Human Affairs Research Centers
Seattle, Washington

Albert Eglash
Psychologist in Private Practice
San Luis Obispo, California

Gilbert Geis
Department of Social Ecology
University of California
Irvine, California

John Harding
Devon Probation and After-Care Service
Exeter, Devon
United Kingdom

Bruce Jacob
College of Law
Ohio State University
Columbus, Ohio

Laura Nader
Department of Anthropology
University of California
Berkeley, California

Kathleen Smith
Cylnnog Caernarvon
North Wales
United Kingdom

John Stookey
Department of Political Science
Arizona State University
Tempe, Arizona

About the Editors

Joe Hudson received the Ph.D. (social work; sociology) from the University of Minnesota. He is Director of Comprehensive Planning for the Minnesota Department of Corrections and has previously worked with the Department as Director of Research and Development and as Director of the Minnesota Restitution Center. Dr. Hudson has had previous professional experience working in an adult prison, a diagnostic center for juvenile offenders, and a residential treatment center for children. He has been a faculty member at the School of Social Development, University of Minnesota—Duluth and at the School of Social Work, University of Minnesota—Minneapolis. Dr. Hudson is co-author of *Considering the Victim* (1975) and *Community Corrections: Selected Readings* (1976); he has also published numerous articles in the areas of restitution and evaluation research in scientific and professional journals.

Burt Galaway has the M.S. degree (social work) from Columbia University and is a candidate for the Ph.D. degree (social work; sociology) from the University of Minnesota. He has had professional experiences in child welfare and corrections and has been a past director of the Minnesota Restitution Center. Mr. Galaway is currently a faculty member at the School of Social Development, University of Minnesota—Duluth and has had previous teaching experience at the School of Social Work, University of Minnesota—Minneapolis and at Mount Mercy College, Cedar Rapids, Iowa. He is a co-author of *Social Work Processes* (1975), *Considering the Victim* (1975), and *Community Corrections: Selected Readings* (1976). Mr. Galaway has published numerous articles in the areas of child welfare, restitution, and victim compensation in professional journals.